The Tribal Basis
of American Life

Children playing in Olney schoolyard. Photo by Karen Vered. Courtesy of Judith Goode.

THE TRIBAL BASIS
OF AMERICAN LIFE

Racial, Religious, and
Ethnic Groups in Conflict

Edited by
MURRAY FRIEDMAN
and
NANCY ISSERMAN

Foreword by
STEPHEN STEINLIGHT

PRAEGER

Westport, Connecticut
London

Library of Congress Cataloging-in-Publication Data

The tribal basis of American life : racial, religious, and ethnic
   groups in conflict / edited by Murray Friedman and Nancy Isserman ;
   foreword by Stephen Steinlight.
      p. cm.
   Includes bibliographical references and index.
   ISBN 0–275–95970–8 (alk. paper)
      1. Group identity—United States—Congresses.   2. United States—
   Race relations—Congresses.   3. United States—Ethnic relations—
   Congresses.   4. Social groups—United States—Congresses.
   I. Friedman, Murray, 1926 –   .   II. Isserman, Nancy, 1951–   .
   HM131.T678   1998
   305.8'00973—dc21   97–34752

British Library Cataloguing in Publication Data is available.

Library of Congress Catalog Card Number: 97–34752
ISBN: 0–275–95970–8

First published in 1998

Praeger Publishers, 88 Post Road West, Westport, CT 06881
An imprint of Greenwood Publishing Group, Inc.

Printed in the United States of America

The paper used in this book complies with the
Permanent Paper Standard issued by the National
Information Standards Organization (Z39.48–1984).

10 9 8 7 6 5 4 3 2 1

Contents

PART IV.   THE WORLD SETTING AND RESPONSE

A photographic essay follows page 88.

Foreword

From a variety of perspectives, the distinguished essayists in this volume address what are arguably the central social/cultural questions of our time: will the American experiment of creating a cohesive society out of an increasingly diverse population succeed or fail? Is the fabric of American society being riven beyond repair by demographic transformation; historic and contemporary racial/ethnic grievances and conflict; cultural separatism and identity politics; the *kulturkampf* over values, family and gender; and rising religious sectarianism *or* is the rhetoric of social disintegration a needlessly threatening conceptual language to describe processes of demographic, social and cultural change that have defined, reinvented and invigorated American life from the beginning? Are we shooting Niagara or terrifying ourselves with a Chimera of our own creation?

The Tribal Basis of American Life grew out of a 1994 conference supported by a grant from the Pew Charitable Trusts which was a joint project of the Myer and Rosaline Feinstein Center for American Jewish History at Temple University, the Balch Institute for Ethnic Studies and the American Jewish Committee (AJC). The exploration of questions arising from ethnic, social, and religious tensions in American society has been a central activity of the American Jewish Committee for some thirty years. Beginning in the late 1960s under the leadership of Irving M. Levine, AJC pioneered the field of intergroup relations in the United States. From the founding of the Institute for American Pluralism, currently known as the Arthur and Rochelle Belfer Center for American Pluralism, AJC has produced knowledge and understanding that have significantly influenced social scientists and community leaders on the issues of race, ethnicity, pluralism, and identity. We continue to explore issues that the essays in the book address that have arisen from the dramatic changes in demography, in the economy, and in American society that have occurred in the twentieth century. One key question on which our work has increasingly been focused is whether particular ethnic, racial, and religious loyalties have caused Americans to forsake a larger sense of national belonging and allegiance.

George Eliot told us long ago "there is no private life which has not been determined by a wider public life." The social forces discussed in *The Tribal Basis of American Life* affect the lives of millions of Americans today, and new patterns of immigration and internal migration guarantee they will affect millions more in the years ahead. These forces are re-creating the social landscape which serves as both stage and backdrop on and against which our individual and communal lives play out. Nothing is more critical to the future of the national life than understanding these forces and creating conceptual systems and practical mechanisms to address them, including those "rules of the game" to which Friedman alludes in his essay. It is our hope that this book will be of considerable help in that challenging endeavor.

Dr. Stephen Steinlight
Director, National Affairs
American Jewish Committee

I

Introduction

1

The Tribal Basis of American Life

Murray Friedman

The fewer answers the era of rational knowledge provides to the basic questions of human beings, the more deeply it would seem people . . . cling to the ancient certainties of their tribe.

—*Vaclav Havel*

Vaclav Havel's comment springs not only from conflicts that have torn his native Czechoslovakia apart and caused it to disappear as a nation but from divisions that exist in the broader society. Here in the United States we are witnessing a startling increase in racial, ethnic, and religious tensions that reflect important, perhaps even fundamental, changes in American life.

Divisions along these lines, of course, are hardly new. Anti-Catholic and anti-immigrant feeling as well as racial violence have always been with us. Throughout the first half of the twentieth century, however, they tended to be submerged by broader social and economic issues. During the Great Depression, conflict more often than not revolved around clashes between capital and labor. Liberals and conservatives argued (as they do today) about the role of government in improving the lives of people.[1] In the postwar years, many celebrated the demise of Western imperialism as hitherto exploited darker skinned peoples, exercising their newfound sense of nationality, moved out from under the control of their economic masters.

Yet race and ethnicity were never far from public consciousness. Liberals mounted campaigns against anti-Semitism and racial injustice in the 1950s and 1960s and were joined by conservatives. These efforts were subsumed, however, within a broader attempt to expand opportunities to ever larger numbers of Americans. In the post–World War II years, an ideology of racial equality began to take shape. Swedish sociologist Gunnar Myrdal and his associates, who had been commissioned by the Carnegie Foundation to study race relations here, argued in *The American Dilemma* (1944) that Americans were uncomfortable with the contradiction between their democratic ideals and their daily practices of racial discrimination, a contradiction that would inevitably lead to change.

They were proven right. Before long, plays, films, public schools, and interfaith organizations began to teach that racial and religious differences were only skin deep in contrast to the things that all people held in common. The Anti-Defamation League sent Bess Myerson, the first Jewish Miss America, around the country to warn that one could not be beautiful and hate.

What focused the nation's attention on issues of racial injustice most centrally, however, was the 1954 Supreme Court decision banning segregated public schools. The early successes of the civil rights movement spearheaded by the Rev. Martin Luther King, Jr., and others created a sense of optimism that the nation was finally coming to grips with prejudice and discrimination. The creation of the United Nations following the war against Nazism also seemed to promise that the nations of the world were at long last joining together to wipe out the twin scourges of group hatred and war.

As we move toward the close of the twentieth century, however, the high hopes of the postwar years have been shattered. In the 1990s, we watched with mounting horror massacres of Tutsis and Hutus in Rwanda, the intensification of civil war along ethnic and religious lines in the former Soviet Union, and tribal warfare between Croats and Serbs and Bosnian Muslims in what was Yugoslavia. Seemingly in every part of the world, nationalism and religious fundamentalism were on the rise, bringing in their wake terrorism, assassinations, and widespread human rights violations. What had proved painfully evident, as Sir Isaiah Berlin wrote in an essay in the *Partisan Review* in 1978, was that nationalism had become the dominant political force of the century.

Nor was the West spared such conflict as was evident in clashes between Roman Catholics and Protestants in Northern Ireland, language disputes in Belgium and efforts on the part of French-speaking Quebec to declare its independence from Canada.[2] Here in the United States, despite homogenizing influences like television and other modern technologies, regional differences persist, reminding us of William Faulkner's comment that in the South, the past is never dead, "it isn't even past."[3] Moreover, as James Davison Hunter and Kimon Howland Sargeant report in Chapter 3, here we are encountering a rise in what they call culture wars.

What has held this country together has been a common set of ideas embodied in the Declaration of Independence and the Constitution. Culture, religion, and ethnicity have divided us, to be sure, but our political and constitutional beliefs, built around the idea of protecting the rights of the individual, provided the glue much of the time. Until massive immigration at the turn of the twentieth century and for perhaps a half century thereafter, the various racial and religious groups were presided over by what the late University of Pennsylvania sociologist E. Digby Baltzell called *The Protestant Establishment*.[4] Whatever limitations this "charter group" placed on ethnic outsiders—its failures were especially egregious in the treatment of African Americans and American Indians—it provided a unifying force. Indeed, the genius of the Protestant Establishment, Baltzell argued, was its ability to incorporate ethnic outsiders by opening opportunities and status to increasingly larger numbers, even as it managed to preserve its own power and primacy.

In the years since the passage of liberalized immigration legislation in 1965, the demographic portrait of this country has undergone vast changes. The big winners in the new immigration sweepstakes are of Asian and Latin American origin. The Asian population, estimated at 9 million in 1997, is expected to rise to 12 million by the year 2000 and to triple by 2050. Hispanic Americans (sometimes referred to as Latinos) number over 29 million people today and will rise to some 42 million by 2013, or slightly more than the estimated 42 million blacks; they are expected to grow to 81 million in 2050.[5] Meanwhile, the black population, while trailing behind Hispanics, will be growing sharply as well—from 32 million in 1997 to an estimated 62 million in 2050. The distribution of many of these newcomers is uneven, it should be noted, tending to concentrate group conflict in a few states and largely urban areas and giving a geographic dimension to our current divisions.

These dramatic demographic and social divisions coincide with broader changes in our society. Earlier immigrants arrived at a time when the economy rested on a manufacturing base which was able to integrate people with few or no skills. Our current high-tech and service-oriented society operating in a global economy offers fewer opportunities for newcomers. Also starting in the 1960s and spurred in part by the civil rights and race revolutions, we have witnessed a rise in group assertiveness. Women, gays, and American Indians, as well as blacks, began to challenge the barriers they faced and to seek group remedies. In this they were joined by many young people of all ethnic backgrounds who protested against the war in Vietnam and sought a greater degree of personal freedom.

Many new or newly emerging groups insist that building group pride and solidarity and obtaining greater economic and political power are more important than the goal of integration, or at least are a prerequisite to gaining full equality.[6] This emphasis on group in contrast with an earlier emphasis on individual rights and responsibilities—which formed the earlier social contract from the adoption of the Constitution through the first half of the twentieth century—has reinforced the group or tribal dimension in American life.

In a society that has always been obsessed with race, it is important to note that most of the contemporary immigrants are nonwhite. Whites in the coming years will account for a declining share of the population, reaching a peak of perhaps 208 million in 2029.[7]

Until comparatively recently, the attention of most Americans has been on conflicts growing out of racial divisions rather than on ethnic or religious particularities, a view reinforced by the United States Census and the Department of Labor, which classify Americans mostly by race. Programs of multiculturalism in schools and universities also place a heavy emphasis on race (and, in recent years, gender).[8]

Religion, however, continues to play a powerful force in American life.[9] Among the most striking of the religious trends in recent years has been the growth of more conservative church groups at a time when mainstream, mainly eastern Protestant bodies, such as the Episcopal Church, the United Church of Christ, the Presbyterian Church (USA), and the United Methodist Church—groups that helped shape and unify the American social as well as religious landscape throughout our history—have been declining.[10] The Muslim population is growing as well—to an estimated four million members in 1997. By the close of the twentieth century, there will be more Muslims in this country than Jews and Episcopalians.[11] Contrasting visions among these religious bodies as to what is right and wrong and on broader social economic issues have added enormously to the conflicts that wrack our society.

Nor do denominations alone, as Hunter and Sargeant note in Chapter 3, define our divisions. For the values often found within conservative religious groups cross denominational lines and link up with "parachurch" bodies. A "Moral Majority" or "Christian Right," usually seen as most closely associated with evangelical Protestant movements, also includes more traditional Jews and some Roman Catholics. De facto alliances have also been formed by liberal Protestant religious bodies with secular movements such as People for the American Way, National Organization of Women (NOW), and the American Humanist Association. So bitter, in fact, are feelings engendered over issues like abortion, Hunter and Sargeant declare, that these "orthodox" and "progressive" alliances often do not operate even on the same plane of moral discourse. There are also growing and bitter divisions within religious bodies as, for example, collisions between certain Orthodox and Reform Jewish groups over who is a Jew or between liberal and conservative Roman Catholics on the right of women to undertake religious functions within the Church that add to fragmentation.

Given the limitations faced by religio-ethnic outsiders and those who feel themselves aggrieved, this is hardly surprising. What has caught many by surprise, however, is the newfound sense of group identity and assertiveness of those seen as long integrated into American society, including descendants of turn-of-the-century migrations. Bumper stickers proudly announce Italian, Ukrainian, and other identifications. Many Jews who had eagerly sought assimilation—and found their entry into the society speeded by doing so—now look back with nostalgia to an earlier immigrant past. Indeed, religious orthodoxy usually associated with that period, has been revived among American-born Jews, and even the more assimilated give indications of turning inward as a result of threats to Israel's safety and security and recent collisions with blacks at home.

Most startling has been the entrance into the political arena of a variously estimated 30 to 50 million Protestant evangelicals to battle for their values and style of life felt to be threatened by recent currents of thought and behavior. These groups retreated from an earlier foray into politics into a preoccupation with personal salvation in the 1920s following defeats on such issues as the teaching of evolution and prohibition. Since the 1970s, however, under names like the Moral Majority and Christian Coalition, many have reentered the public arena to press for the restoration of some form of prayer and Bible reading in the schools and to oppose efforts to legitimatize what they see as newer forms of sexual morality.

Joining them on some fronts has been the Roman Catholic church as well as some Orthodox Jews. The Church had never left the political arena, having in the postwar years opposed abortion reform and campaigned for government aid to parochial schools. During the 1980s and 1990s, however, it stepped up its efforts to influence public policy on attempts to teach about homosexuality and distribute condoms in the public schools. In turn, liberal Protestants, most Jews, and civil liberties groups have recoiled from such pressures. They fear that a "Christian Right," operating through what has been seen as "stealth" and other antidemocratic methods and skillfully using television and radio to reach millions in their appeals, are threatening the foundations of democratic society.

In his seminal *Culture Wars: The Struggle to Define America*, James Davison Hunter warned that something very new and deeply troubling was happening in American life. In the postwar years, he pointed out, anti-Semitism had declined among evangelicals. There was growing tolerance among Protestants, Catholics, Jews, Mormons, and others that coincided with a slow and steady expansion of political and ideological tolerance toward Communists, atheists, blacks, Hispanics, homosexuals, and those cohabiting outside of marriage. Hunter now saw—and many agreed—that a major realignment had occurred. This realignment was more than a social referendum over the policies of Richard Nixon and Ronald Reagan. It was caused by fundamentally different conceptions of moral authority—of what constitutes the truth and the good society and one's obligations to neighbors and to the community itself.[12]

As we move to the close of the twentieth century, we find a society driven by group claims and increasingly at war with itself on a wide variety of fronts.

Item: Black Muslims in the Philadelphia schools petitioned the school board in 1993 that the practice of closing schools for Christian and Jewish holidays be extended to the Moslem faith.

Item: One out of every eight public school students in New York City in 1993—a total of 125,000—was taking either bilingual education or English as a second language at a time when legislatures in Florida, Arizona, and California had passed amendments to state constitutions declaring English the official language.[13]

Item: In 1992, New York City found itself polarized for weeks and its school chancellor ousted as the Roman Catholic archdiocese and a number of Protestant groups objected to the adoption by the school board of a curriculum that included the study of AIDS, sex education, and the teaching of acceptance of homosexual lifestyles.

Item: Following adoption by the school district of Portland, Oregon in 1987 of an Afrocentric curriculum intended to acquaint U.S. blacks with their long-ignored African heritage, school systems in Atlanta, Detroit, Fort Lauderdale, and other cities have incorporated such curriculum aids in school programs. The Portland approach came under attack by liberal critics, including historian Arthur Schlesinger, Jr., who saw these efforts at multiculturalism as bringing about what he called in a book, *The Disuniting of America*.

Item: In August 1994, South Carolina was embroiled in a controversy as a group of black legislators insisted that the Confederate flag should not fly atop state buildings.[14]

Item: Early in 1994, state attorneys in courts in North Carolina, Florida, Texas, and Louisiana argued before the Supreme Court that the *Shaw v. Reno* decision the previous year did not apply to their states. This case had declared that redistricting legislation that set up gerrymandered voting districts aimed at electing black representatives was constitutionally suspect. Since then the Court has made such redistricting more difficult.[15]

Item: On September 7, 1994, the Justice Department filed a brief in a Piscataway, New Jersey, case arguing that in a situation involving two teachers hired at the same time, it is legal during a budget cutback to fire the white teacher (who happened to be Jewish) over a black teacher because of her race. On August 8, 1996, the U.S. Third Circuit Court of Appeals declared this action unlawful.[16] More recently, the Clinton administration has backed away from the earlier Justice Department position.

Item: Saying that it might cost her reelection, Senator Diane Feinstein, on October 21, 1994, declared her opposition to a hotly disputed California ballot proposal aimed at controlling the flood of illegal immigrants across the state's southern border. She barely survived, even as the anti-immigration proposal, Proposition 187, won overwhelmingly in the referendum.

Item: On October 5, 1994, Paul J. Hill, a former Presbyterian minister and abortion protestor, was convicted (and later sentenced to execution) on federal charges of killing two people and wounding a third in an attempt to thwart legal abortions at a clinic in Pensacola, Florida.[17]

The foregoing suggest that Americans are being asked to deal with situations that were rarely thought of a generation ago. Is it constitutional or at least reasonable public policy to provide governmental vouchers to enable parents to send their children to parochial schools, as the Roman Catholic church and certain Orthodox Jewish and other religious groups insist? Can a state permit an all-religious school district to be established? In the Kiryas Joel case in June 1994, the U.S. Supreme Court held such a school district to be unconstitutional, yet New York legislators have been seeking to modify the law to permit this. Should only blacks make movies about blacks, a position taken by director Spike Lee (known especially for the film *Malcolm X*)?[18] Is it in the best interest of blacks or the community generally for Mississippi Valley State University, an almost all-black university, to go to court to challenge its merger with a nearby white school? The impetus for the merger was a 1992 Supreme Court ruling holding that thirty years after the Brown school desegregation decision, the state's higher education system was still segregated.[19]

These questions leave Americans confused. The lessons we thought we had learned a generation or two ago on how to make a diverse society work appear to provide less reliable guides today. At the height of the civil rights revolution in the 1960s, it was felt that overcoming governmentally sponsored discriminatory barriers would result in fuller inclusion of minorities into society at all levels. For some it has. But in the late 1990s the condition of large numbers of blacks and other racial outsiders has deteriorated. This has led some policy makers to institute special remedial and open enrollment programs in colleges like City College in New York to enhance the possibilities of minority group students, moves that others argue only lower educational standards without providing much assistance to those enrolled in such programs.[20]

The premise of this country's long battle against prejudice and discrimination was that human rights are indivisible. We are aware now that some of our most recent conflicts are between minorities. This was illustrated most vividly in the Los Angeles rioting in 1992, following which Rodney King asked his haunting question of whether Americans can learn to live together. Jonathan Rieder and Gary Okihiro report in Chapter 4 and 5, respectively, that a number of our recent collisions have been between Asians and blacks, Hispanics and blacks, and blacks and Jews. In the passage of California anti-immigration Proposition 187, exit polls showed that close to a majority of California's African-American community, long a bellwether on issues of racial justice, voted "yes," causing syndicated columnist William Raspberry, who is black, to wonder whether minorities need enemies or at least think they do (which amounts to the same thing) to serve as the glue that holds them together.[21]

Some have come to question the ability of our political system to deal with these problems. A University of Chicago survey in 1994 found support growing among African Americans for the creation of a separate black political party. According to Michael Dawson, the political scientist who conducted the survey, of more than 1200 blacks polled in 1988, 26 percent supported a separate party. By 1994, he found the black community evenly divided. Paul Hill, the abortion protestor and murderer, represents a tiny minority in the pro-life movement, but there is evidence of growing political restlessness in Catholic and conservative Christian circles. An editorial in the *Catholic Standard and Times* in Philadelphia warns, "If the Democratic Party continues its endorsement of abortion and if the GOP tent gets 'big enough' to house pro-choice sentiments, Americans with pro-life beliefs will find it increasingly difficult to fit into a two-party system."[22]

It is unlikely that such political fragmentation will take place—at least for the foreseeable future. What we are seeing, however, perhaps for the first time in our history, is the open recognition and even acceptance of the retribalization of America. Some wonder whether we are witnessing the seeds of another Bosnia sprouting up all around us. Of course, such divisiveness does not go unchallenged. Increasing discussion over how these forces are to be reconciled and the common identity assured make up much of our political discourse today. Still, the discussion is so new and feelings run so deep, as Nathan Glazer suggests in Chapter 9, that we have not found a common language in which to talk about these issues.

The fact is that we are literally at the beginning of our understanding of the dynamics of modern group life and of how group identity in this country affects us. We get some hint of this in studies such as Ivan Light's *Ethnic Enterprise in the United States* and Susan Tennenbaum's *A Credit to Their Community: Jewish Loan Societies in the United States*, which deal with how communal support systems help groups to rise in our society. Judith Goode in Chapter 7 describes how diverse groups usually seen at loggerheads with one another in their neighborhoods have come together in one section of Philadelphia to deal with common problems in the schools and drug addiction. We need to know much more than we do now about "the rules of the game" by which groups work out their different status.

It would be naive, however, to suggest, as James Hunter cautions in *Culture Wars* in discussing differences over religio-cultural beliefs, that some bland consensus can be reached that will reconcile contending parties. The divisions over such explosive issues as abortion or even the various definitions of affirmative action, for example, are firm and seemingly unyielding. What may be attainable, he suggests, would be to learn "how to contend over the moral differences that divide."[23]

Even as we wrestle with these problems it is important to point out we have been and continue to remain a successful society if we measure success, as James Kurth suggests in Chapter 8, not by some abstract ideal but by the experiences of multigroup societies in other parts of the world. The fact is that, despite our problems, people continue to come to the United States and in great numbers. Immigration accounts for some 37 percent of our current population growth.[24]

We are successful, also, in that, unlike in many parts of the world, for the most part we discuss and argue about deeply divisive issues rather than resort to violence. Given the bewildering array of peoples who have found their way to these shores and live and interact with one another—more than two hundred Protestant denominations, Catholics, Jews, whites and blacks, Italians, Poles, Slovaks, and other white ethnics as well as newly emerging social groupings—we have here all the elements of a society posed to self-destruct. Still, with the single exception of our bloody Civil War, we have managed somehow to hold the country together and, over time, bring outsiders in as equal partners.[25]

The system, of course, does not always work. Racial minorities continue to remain outsiders. If we recall, however, how our society behaved at the turn of the twentieth century when millions of newcomers were flooding into the country or as recently as a generation and a half ago in the South and elsewhere in this country, we have come a long way. We have witnessed the breakdown of institutional segregation, the emergence of a sizable black middle class, increased movement of minorities into higher education, and the election and appointment of minorities to political and other important positions in American life.

When we look closely we can also see that many recent newcomers are reenacting the experiences of earlier European immigrants. Francis Fukuyama's statistics on family values and stability among newer immigrants are impressive. Using Census Bureau figures, he reports that 78 percent of Asian and Pacific island households in this country are family households as opposed to 70 percent of white Americans and that while Asians are equally likely to be married as whites, they are only half as likely to be divorced.[26]

The latest influx of peoples is different in racial background from the immigration of the turn of the century, which long ago overcame the bitter xenophobia and bigotry it inspired and is best remembered today almost with nostalgia. For all the current furor over newcomers, our history suggests, as Gary Rubin points out in Chapter 2, that this backlash will ultimately recede as the new immigrants adapt to the broader American culture and as our society changes through exposure to them.

Some, of course, see blacks and Latinos as one vast underclass. Indeed, Puerto Ricans and others have brought serious economic problems with them. But it is important to remember that the 22 million Latinos are a highly diverse group. Latinos of Cuban and Mexican origin (who constitute 65 percent of the Hispanic community) have a 50 percent lower rate of female-headed homes than do Puerto Ricans, while Mexican Americans often have stronger family structures than do whites because of strong taboos on smoking, drinking, and drug use during pregnancy.[27]

This country's extraordinary diversity, therefore, need not be seen only as a series of "problems." As Judith Goode and her team of anthropologists note from their investigations of the Olney and Kensington sections of Philadelphia, day-to-day relations among different groups involve accommodation and cooperation as well as conflict. This suggests that the tribal basis of American life can also be a source of strength, adding vigor and variety to our society. It is something we should feel proud of even as we go about the daunting task of finding out how to make one nation out of many peoples.

This book is an outgrowth of a conference held in 1994 sponsored by the Myer and Rosaline Feinstein Center for American Jewish History, Temple University, in cooperation with the Balch Institute for Ethnic Studies and the Philadelphia Chapter of the American Jewish Committee under grants from the Pew Charitable Trusts and the Pennsylvania Humanities Council. We are grateful to these organizations and the scholars participating in the conference for helping to explore current ethnic, religious, and racial conflicts. John Tenhula of Balch played a key role in helping to plan and fund the conference, as did Gary Rubin, then director of the National Domestic Affairs Department of the American Jewish Committee, which also provided financial support. Several of the chapters included here were commissioned later. We leave for another day the attempt to develop what might be called "the rules of the game," the effort to discuss more fully how Americans can confront and learn how to resolve some of these divisive issues. It is our hope that the present volume will be helpful to general readers, specialists in the field, and students who seek to understand the increasingly tribal basis of American life.

NOTES

1. Gary Gerstley, "The Protean Character of American Liberalism," *American Historical Review* (October 1994): 1043–73.

2. See also Samuel P. Huntington, *The Clash of Civilizations and the Remaking of World Order* (New York: Simon & Schuster, 1996).

3. See Peter Applebome, *Dixie Rising: How the South is Shaping American Values* (New York: Times Books, 1996).

4. *Aristocracy & Caste in America* (New York: Random House, 1964).

5. *New York Times*, December 5, 1992; *Philadelphia Inquirer*, October 14, 1997.

6. See Stokely Carmichael and Charles V. Hamilton, *Black Power: The Politics of Liberation in America* (New York: Vintage Books, 1967); Harold Cruse, *The Crisis of the Negro Intellectual* (New York: William Morrow & Company, 1967).

7. Alejandro Portes and Min Zhou, "The New Second Generation: Segmented Assimilation and Its Variants," *The Annals of The American Academy of Political and Social Science*, November 1993, p. 22; Diana L. Eck, "Old Glory Flies Over Many Religions," *Philadelphia Inquirer*, July 4, 1992; *New York Times*, December 4, 1992.

8. Jonathan Sarna, "The Secret of Jewish Continuity," *Commentary* (October 1994): 55–59.

9. According to a recent study conducted by a professor of governmental studies at Notre Dame, among whites who are members of Christian denominations, the Republican party has become the home of regular churchgoers, including Roman Catholics. The analysis prepared by David C. Leege also indicates that white voters who attend church irregularly or declare themselves as irreligious cast Democratic majorities.

10. Sarna, "The Secret of Jewish Continuity," p. 57; Dean M. Kelley, *Why Conservative Churches Are Growing: A Study in Sociology of Religion* (New York: Harper & Row, 1977); *New York Times*, September 25, 1994.

11. *International Herald Tribune*, January 11, 1994. John Green, Lyman Kellstedt, James Guth, and Corwin Smidt, "Who Elected Clinton? A Collision of Values," *First Things* (August/September 1997): 35–40. Significantly, the New York City Board of Education in 1997 settled a court suit by agreeing to

encourage schools to display the Muslim star and crescent symbol as part of displays containing symbols of Christmas, Hanukkah, and other holidays (*New York Times*, June 14, 1997).

12. James Davison Hunter, *Culture Wars: The Struggle to Define America* (New York: Basic Books, 1990), pp. 39–40, 49.

13. *Philadelphia Inquirer*, May 18, 1993, and November 29, 1996; *New York Times*, January 4, 1993.

14. *New York Times*, August 22, 1994.

15. Ibid., March 21, 1994; Elaine R. Jones, "In Peril: Black Lawmakers," *New York Times*, September 11, 1994, and December 19, 1996.

16. Jeffrey Rosen, "Is Affirmative Action Doomed?" *The New Republic*, October 17, 1994, pp. 25–34; *Philadelphia Daily News*, August 9, 1996.

17. *New York Times*, October 6, 1994.

18. *New York Times*, March 28, 1994.

19. *New York Times*, May 9, 1994.

20. James Traub, *City on a Hill: Testing the American Dream at City College* (New York: Addison-Wesley, 1994).

21. *Philadelphia Tribune*, November 25, 1994; Jeffrey Goldberg, "The Overachiever," *New York*, April 10, 1995, pp. 43–51; William Raspberry, *Philadelphia Inquirer*, September 23, 1994.

22. *Philadelphia Inquirer*, September 29, 1994.

23. James Hunter, *The Struggle to Define America* (New York: Basic Books, 1991), p. 318.

24. For a recent critique of this country's immigration policies, see Peter Brimelow, *Alien Nation: Common Sense about America's Immigration Disaster* (New York: Random House, 1995).

25. James Hunter, *Before the Shooting Begins: Searching for Democracy in America's Culture War* (New York: Free Press, 1994), p. 4.

26. Peter I. Rose, " 'Of Every Hue and Caste': Race, Immigration, and Perceptions of Pluralism," *The Annals*, (November 1993), 198; Francis Fukuyama, "Immigrants and Family Values," *Commentary* (May 1993): 28.

27. Fukuyama, "Immigrants and Family Values," p. 29.

II

The Changing American Group Setting

2

Immigration, Pluralism, and Public Policy

Gary E. Rubin

As we look around the world today at places riven by ethnic conflict as far flung as Bosnia, Rwanda, Iraq, and Sri Lanka, Americans can take pride in the pluralism that characterizes our society. But, we cannot be complacent. Each of these examples demonstrates that ethnic conflict can be enduring and violent, sometimes surfacing after years of dormancy. If we wish to preserve the strength of our pluralism, we need to pay constant attention to ethnic trends in American society and ways to enhance mutual respect and cooperation.

Pluralism in the American context involves both respect for group identity and the expectation that various ethnic communities will interact in positive and mutually cooperative ways. We join our separate groups to express our deepest identities, but when we interact in public, it is on the basis of rational principles that all groups, no matter what their particular ideologies, can accept. Within our communities, we seek to continue particular heritages, but as a society as a whole, we are all citizens with common obligations, sharing a public life to which each community contributes.[1]

In the midst of global challenge to the very notion of peacefully interacting ethnicities, how can we preserve this notion of pluralism today? Approaching this issue requires an understanding of how waves of immigration at different periods of American history have interacted with the host society and the consequent various strategies that were and are needed to protect and promote pluralism.

In the 1970s, work on pluralism in the United States focused on the identities of European ethnic groups that had migrated to this country around the turn of the twentieth century and were at that point entering their third generation of residence in America. The central questions were how salient their ethnicity remained as part of their basic identities and how could their ethnic allegiances contribute to the strength of the larger society. Proponents of pluralism argued their case on the basis of two central assumptions, one of which was highly contested, the other enjoying widespread support.

The first assumption of ethnic pluralists of the 1970s was that ethnic identity was a strong and enduring component of an individual's personality. Even though Americans of Italian, Greek, Polish, or Eastern European Jewish descent were by then entering into their third or even fourth generation of life in the United States, much of their outlook and behavior could still be explained by their ethnic origin. Irving Levine, longtime director of the American Jewish Committee's Institute on Pluralism and Group Identity was fond of telling audiences that, "Ethnicity is as deep as sex and death." Moreover, Levine argued that if white ethnicity were not given public and political expression at a time of heightened black consciousness, it would surface in negative and antagonistic ways, such as the presidential campaigns of George Wallace. To respond to this threat, Levine and his supporters called for a positive program to recognize the importance of ethnicity and to allow it constructive expression.[2]

This ethnic pluralism came under vigorous challenge by scholars and activists who doubted the lasting salience of ethnicity as successive generations became more entrenched in America. To them, assimilation was the inevitable fate of the grandchildren and great-grandchildren of immigrants. Any remaining vestiges of ethnic identification were merely symbolic. The interests of proponents of this view were not simply scholarly. They believed that class, rather than ethnicity, was the basic building block of American society, and they argued that third generation European ethnics should join their economic peers in seeking greater social and economic justice in the United States.[3]

While Levine and his colleagues built up impressive organizational resources to promote their point of view, this debate was not so much settled as overwhelmed. As analysts were arguing about whether European-based ethnic identity would last, large numbers of Latino, Asian, and Caribbean immigrants were beginning to enter the United States in the 1970s as a result of the landmark Immigration Act of 1965. Further immigration legislation enacted in 1990 assures that for the foreseeable future legal immigration will continue at the rate of about 800,000 admissions per year. Moreover, unlike the European migrations of 80 years ago, the great majority of these newcomers are distinguished from the American mainstream not only by their heritages but also by their racial features. Whatever the fate of European ethnicity, America will be a nation in which ethnic pluralism will remain a central feature in the long run. How to handle ethnic identity has become a permanent challenge.[4]

The second basic assumption of the ethnic pluralists encountered no serious challenges. It was that immigrants and their descendants would interact with American society in a way that would affect both the larger society and the ethnic community. Immigrants might struggle to maintain their identity in America, but their encounter with mainstream institutions and ideas would be dynamic and constant, to their mutual benefit.

No European ethnic group better exemplified this acknowledged "fact" about American pluralism than the Jews. Numerous studies chronicled the evolution of the American Jewish community from immigrant enclave to generator of small business to one of the most professionally, economically, socially, and politically successful groups in America. Geographically, the community moved from urban ghetto to city periphery to suburban settlement. At each stage of the way, a complex set of relationships evolved between the larger society and the American Jewry. Indeed, the saga of the community lay in the encounter between Jews and Americans at large.[5]

Few doubted that whatever their fate in American society, the evolution of American ethnic groups would be decided in intense interaction with the host culture. This was the basic assumption from which all analysis of pluralism began. For proponents of ethnic pluralism, this assumption meant that ethnic identity needed to be nurtured so that it could encounter the broad society from a position of strength. But, the very assumption of interaction has been thrown into question by the latest wave of immigration.

The new immigration that has been entering the United States since the 1970s has developed an acculturation strategy dramatically different from that of its European predecessors. This change has profound implications for the concept of pluralism and the course of intergroup relations in America.

European ethnic groups assumed that pluralism meant intense interaction with the larger society. Advocates of strong group identities believed that ethnic communities needed to develop their self-awareness and political skills precisely so that they could function within a pluralistic society and influence the nature of a multigroup America. There was no thought among the ethnic pluralists that identity meant separation. Rather, identity was a strategy for interacting with others.

The new immigration has not followed this pattern. In many cases, a central feature of its approach to the larger society has been separation rather than integration. Moreover, this has occurred not because of any ideological rejection of pluralism, but, rather, out of the rational pursuit of ethnic group interest.

The key fact about the new immigration is that it is made up of racial and ethnic minorities. Over 40 percent of immigrants since the 1970s are Asian, while another 40 percent come from Latino countries. Immigrants around the turn of the twentieth century were racially indistinct from other Americans though they were culturally different. Today's newcomers are both racially and culturally distinct. Immigrants are likely to be Chinese in San Francisco, Koreans and Mexicans in Los Angeles, Cubans in Miami, or black Caribbeans in New York.

The minority nature of immigrants has two consequences for their relation to American society. First, their acculturation threatens not to be into the mainstream social and economic groups dominated by white Americans but rather into subcultures characterized by economic failure, family disintegration, and social pathology that beset many American minority groups. Second, these new immigrants are likely to encounter the prejudice and discrimination that still plague American minorities.

Facing blockages to mobility arising out of threatened acculturation to unsuccessful groups and ethnic prejudice, new immigrants have often responded by cutting themselves off from the larger society and pursuing social and economic mobility on their own. If their success in the new country is threatened by interaction with it, they have limited their relations with others to be free of the constraints of minority identity in American society. Unlike the previous wave of immigration, for today's newcomers separation rather than integration has become the most rational mobility strategy. Studies of several recent immigrant groups confirm this trend.

Ruben Rumbaut, for example, has examined the acculturation experiences of Indochinese refugees in Southern California. This group suffers from many modes of social pathology. Poverty rates among them are high, they live in poor residential conditions, their welfare utilization rates are well above average, and many cannot find jobs. By most standards, this is a classic underclass population. Yet, two indicators belie this characterization. This same Indochinese population has the lowest infant mortality rate in the area and the lowest rate of neonatal health problems. Students from this community have the highest grade point averages in the public high school. These markers of success are associated with separation from the surrounding community. The more integrated the Indochinese refugees, the more their health rates and school performance converge to the area's norm. It is the Indochinese culture that preserves unusually high health standards and school excellence, despite the community's poverty. When that culture breaks down, these positive traits vanish. In these conditions, the only rational strategy for the Indochinese is to preserve their uniqueness and avoid too much contact with resident groups. Separation rather than integration underlies the success they have been able to achieve in American society.[6]

Much the same considerations shape the acculturation experiences of black Caribbean immigrants to New York. This group has been able to find an employment niche as mid-level workers in the city's service economy, in positions such as data entry personnel, messengers, car service operators, and day care specialists. They have succeeded in maintaining their communal identity through highly public events such as the annual Caribbean Day carnival in Brooklyn, as well as through a network of private social clubs. They have also done quite well in the complex arena of New York's native-born African-American politics. Separation from others who share their racial characteristics rather than integration has been seen by some Caribbeans as essential to their American mobility.[7]

A third example is the Sikh population of northern California. As described by Alejandro Portes and Min Zhou, Sikhs from the Punjab region of India settled in California's farm country, where, despite considerable discrimination from the local ''redneck'' population, they have succeeded in achieving mobility in the agricultural economy of the area. Their children have outperformed native-born students in high school. A key factor in their success was parents' admonition to their children to avoid too much contact with white students and to preserve the family's honor in their personal and academic lives. In this case, both discrimination and self-selection created separation between the Sikh and white groups, which the immigrants saw as an important condition for their success.[8]

Three points underlie the experience of these three recent immigrant groups and others like them. First, within the context of American society, they are all perceived as minority groups. Each has striven to escape the discrimination and low social status often associated with minorities. Second, each has achieved success through social separation from other groups in its area and reliance on its own culture and ethnic resources. Third, each perceived this separation as vital to its long-range mobility.

This recent immigrant mobility strategy turns the experience of European ethnic groups at the turn of the twentieth century on its head. For the European origin communities, debate surfaced about whether a separate identity could be maintained into the third generation and beyond, but no one doubted that these groups would interact intensely with the surrounding society. With recent newcomers, few doubt the lasting distinctiveness of their identity, largely because of their racial characteristics and continuing immigration, but their degree of interaction with their neighbors in American society is very much in doubt.

Is this simply a difference of cultural lifestyles of no real importance to the social health of American society? Do new attitudes and behaviors about interaction make a real difference in prospects for intergroup relations in American society?

The challenge to American pluralism brought about by the drive toward separatism of the new immigration is disturbing for two reasons. First, ethnic conflict is always a danger to a multigroup society, but the threat would appear to be greater where groups fail to develop understanding and respect for one another through constant interaction. It is true that interaction can produce tension where encounters are conflictual, but the expectation of American pluralism has always been that group encounters would take place in an atmosphere of rationality and mutual respect. Despite many instances of conflict, that expectation most often has been met. A society of groups that see mutual separation as a prime condition for success threatens to produce lack of understanding and tolerance that could exacerbate intercommunal tensions that have recently accelerated both in the United States and around the world.

Second, social separation threatens to undermine the positive promise of American pluralism. The American pluralist ethos presumes that groups interacting will stimulate one another to the benefit of all. The ethnic pluralists of the 1970s, for example, believed that ethnic groups would grow stronger as a result of their encounter with American democratic values and that the whole society would gain from each community's preservation of its heritage. These benefits are impossible to realize in the context of social separation. How can pluralistic values be maintained in the era of the new immigration?

Preserving American pluralism today requires the promotion of effective social policies to realize the benefits of cultural interaction while furthering the success and contributions to American society of various ethnic groups. Different approaches to social policy seek to address these challenges, but some handle them more effectively than others.

This problem cannot be effectively addressed, for example, by conservative social policy approaches that rely primarily on the market for a solution to social problems. Recent immigrant groups have chosen a strategy of separation specifically because avoiding interaction best assures their economic success in the minority group conditions of today's America. Relying on the market in this case will simply reinforce social segregation.

An even more harmful policy would seek to reduce or curtail immigration because of the social challenges it poses. It must be remembered that new immigrants have chosen separation to preserve their success in America. This success can be an important factor in revitalizing the country's economy as well as its major cities. The root of the problem is not that immigration is deleterious to American interests. On the contrary, the challenge is how best to incorporate the advantages newcomers bring with them into the larger society. We should not be thinking of how to avoid problems by cutting immigration—that would be a classic case of overreaction to a serious but not insolvable problem—but rather about how to take advantage of newcomers' talents and resources by strengthening American pluralism.[9]

A third counterproductive strategy would be to encourage moves toward greater group separation in American life. Some groups have responded to problems of pluralism by accepting that ethnic communities will never get along in a multigroup society and have therefore promoted strategies to advance their cause in separation from others. They have advanced programs, for example, for using public school curricula to teach primarily about the experience of the groups from which students derive, to allocate jobs by striving to meet quotas based on the ethnic identities of the workforce, and to divide government resources according to the identities of the recipients. Should such programs succeed, the future of pluralism would face great danger.

The social policy strategy best suited for the pluralist future of American society is one that respects the identities and heritages of both new and older American groups and strives to promote equal opportunity for them all as well as continual constructive engagement. What specific programs can advance this goal?

In the realm of education, a constructive program would seek to draw on the heritage of all schoolchildren by encouraging them to explore their various backgrounds in the classroom, at the same time as it teaches values common to all Americans as well as the major historical and cultural themes of the nation of which we are all a part. In higher education, this strategy calls for maintaining the basic core of the canon of great literature while adding to it the significant works of the literatures of newer American groups, which clearly contain wisdom from which all can benefit. The stress throughout should be on both respecting the heritages of all groups that make up America and incorporating them into a broad national cultural framework.[10]

A reasonable pluralistic strategy must also address the workplace. Affirmative action programs that do not rely on rigid quotas or ignore the merit and qualifications of job applicants need to be put in place to assure that minorities do not lose out in workforce decisions simply because of their racial or ethnic identities. The workforce best suited for the national interest is one that is both integrated and qualified. As Americans spend such a major part of their lives on their jobs, social separation simply cannot be overcome without conscious attempts at workplace pluralism.[11]

Of all integrative strategies, probably the most critical is residential integration. Where one lives directly influences many other factors critical to life chances, such as the quality of neighborhood schools, the availability of work within a reasonable commuting distance, access to role models who have successfully negotiated the challenges of American society, and freedom from the constant problems of drugs and crime. The success curves of many ethnic groups will depend in large measure on equal availability of quality living environments.[12]

These strategies will benefit native-born minorities as well. A consistent policy of educational pluralism, affirmative action, and residential integration will redound not only to the benefit of newcomers but to others such as African Americans. That, too, is an important lesson of pluralism. The policies that most effectively advance particular groups are ones that strengthen the entire society.

NOTES

This chapter is dedicated to Irving M. Levine who both inspired and exemplified the ideas in it.

1. On the philosophical underpinnings of democratic pluralism, see John Rawls, *Political Liberalism* (New York: Columbia University Press, 1993).

2. Levine tended to inspire and promote writing by others rather than produce essays or books himself. Works that directly acknowledge his influence include Michael Novak, *The Rise of the Unmeltable Ethnics* (New York: Macmillan, 1971); Andrew M. Greeley, *Why Can't They Be Like Us?* (New York: E. P. Dutton, 1971); and Richard Gambino, *Blood of My Blood* (Garden City, N.Y.: Anchor, 1974).

3. Herbert Gans, "Symbolic Ethnicity," *Ethnic and Racial Studies* II (January 1979); 1–18; Stephen Steinberg, *The Ethnic Myth* (Boston: Beacon Press, 1981).

4. Gary E. Rubin, *Are There Too Many People in the Lifeboat? Immigration and the American Dream* (New York: American Jewish Committee, 1992).

5. Irving Howe, *World of Our Fathers* (New York: Harcourt Brace Jovanovich, 1976); Moses Rischin, *The Promised City* (New York: Harper & Row, 1970); Deborah Dash Moore, *At Home in America* (New York: Columbia University Press, 1981); Sidney Goldstein and Calvin Goldscheider, *Jewish Americans* (Englewood Cliffs, N.J.: Prentice-Hall, 1968).

6. See the San Diego County studies referred to in Alejandro Portes and Ruben Rumbaut, *Immigrant America: A Portrait* (Berkeley: University of California Press, 1990).

7. Philip Kasinitz, *Caribbean New York* (Ithaca, N.Y.: Cornell University Press, 1992).

8. Alejandro Portes and Min Zhou, "The New Second Generation," *Annals of the American Academy of Political and Social Science* 530 (November 1993): 89–91.

9. On the economic contributions, see Thomas Muller, *Immigrants and the American City* (New York: New York University Press, 1993).

10. On the debate on pluralism in the classroom, see Paul Berman, ed., *Debating P.C.* (New York: Laurel, 1992).

11. For a general rationale of affirmative action programs, see Christopher Jencks, "Affirmative Action or Quotas?" in Jencks, ed., *Rethinking Social Policy* (Cambridge, Mass.: Harvard University Press, 1992), pp. 24–69.

12. For a consideration of all of these factors of integration, see Gary Orfield and Carole Ashkinaze, *The Closing Door* (Chicago: University of Chicago Press, 1991).

3

The Religious Roots of the Culture Wars: How Competing Moral Visions Fuel Cultural Conflict

James Davison Hunter and Kimon Howland Sargeant

Religion has always played a central role in American public life. It motivated the Puritans' "errand into the wilderness," justified the abolitionists' battle against slavery, and propelled the popular support for Prohibition. Today, religion animates the public conflicts over prayer in schools, abortion, homosexuality, euthanasia, and family values, to name just a few. To ignore the dynamic import of religion on American history is to miss an important part of our story: religious themes have always played and will continue to play a prominent role in our understanding of who we are as a nation.[1]

The nature of religion's influence upon the public sector, however, is by no means constant or predictable. The role of religion in contemporary public life has undergone a profound transformation that is only beginning to be understood. The controversies over issues ranging from gays in the military to funding for the arts and multiculturalism manifest a deeper argument over what core values and national ideals will be transmitted to the next generation. This debate draws upon fundamentally religious convictions. Take, for example, the issue of abortion, one of the most bitter and divisive conflicts in American public life. While the struggle over abortion may appear to be political in nature, waged primarily in the legislatures and courts, politics alone does not sufficiently explain the vexing nature of the abortion conflict. The very stridency of the battle over abortion reveals that this debate touches upon the vital religious and cultural concerns of the American people. Advocates on either side of the issue pursue their cause not simply out of political pragmatism, but out of a zealous, even quasireligious, devotion. Such fervor and passion is fueled by one's deepest held beliefs. Pro-choice organizations, for example, denounce their opponents for infringing upon a woman's fundamental right to privacy and personal autonomy, while pro-life groups condemn the violent ''murder'' of millions of innocent children. Both sides claim a non-negotiable right—the inviolability of personal autonomy or the sanctity of human life—as the basis for their actions. As a result, the dispute over abortion is nothing less than a battle over two groups' fundamentally different understandings of moral authority—of what is right or wrong, good or bad, American or un-American.

The cleavages at the heart of the contemporary culture war, as demonstrated by the ongoing battles over abortion, are created by what can be called the impulse toward orthodoxy and the impulse toward progressivism. Though these terms are imprecise, they serve as a useful shorthand for describing the particular locus of moral truth, informing the fundamental (although perhaps subconscious) moral allegiances of actors on both sides of the culture war. Conservative individuals—opponents of abortion, proponents of prayer in schools, and the like—are influenced by an orthodox worldview. What defines this orthodoxy is the commitment on the part of adherents to an external, definable, and transcendent authority. The sources of orthodoxy can be the Bible for Evangelical Protestants, the Magisterium of the Church for conservative Catholics, the Talmud for Orthodox Jews, and even forms of Natural Law for some secularists. In contrast, liberal or progressive individuals—proponents of abortion rights and gay rights among others—are influenced by a progressivist worldview. What all progressivist worldviews share in common is the tendency to resymbolize historic faiths according to the prevailing assumptions of contemporary life. Binding moral authority tends to reside not in an external, unchanging transcendent but, instead, in personal experience or scientific rationality or in either of these in conversation with particular religious or cultural traditions. The contours of these opposing worldviews will be discussed subsequently in more detail. Suffice it to say for now that the result of the current cultural realignment, based on these two diametrically opposed worldviews, is, to put it bluntly, a culture war over the meaning of America itself.

Perhaps this characterization, this description of a "battle" over religious and cultural matters, may strike the reader as somewhat extreme. After all, we are a religiously diverse nation and, given this remarkable religious diversity, our nation has been relatively free of conflicts that are defined primarily by religious categories. Catholics and Protestants do not engage in a bloody struggle for power here as they do in Northern Ireland. The "ethnic cleansing" so gruesomely visited upon the people of the former Yugoslavia is virtually unimaginable to us because it draws upon religious and nationalistic animosities that are the antithesis of the tolerance upon which our nation prides itself.

Yet religious conflict has not been absent from American history. Anti-Catholic prejudice was prominent in the nineteenth century, igniting the great school wars of mid-century and contributing to the development of anti-Catholic political parties such as the Know-Nothing party in the 1850s. More than a century later, John F. Kennedy's purported loyalty to Rome became an important political issue in his presidential candidacy. Catholicism has not been the only target of religious intolerance. Other religious minorities have also faced considerable opposition from the Protestant establishment during the nineteenth and much of the twentieth century de facto. Certainly they have many stories to tell of their struggles to carve out a place for themselves in Protestant-dominated America.

One key feature of the American religious landscape up through the 1960s was that it tended to be defined by the differences between religious groups—Puritans v. Quakers, Protestants v. Catholics, and even between different Protestant groups such as Baptists and Lutherans. Denominational identity was closely linked with personal identity. The social and personal significance of religious affiliation is illustrated by Will Herberg's *Protestant-Catholic-Jew*, a classic examination of religious relations in the United States. "The outstanding feature of the religious situation in America today," wrote Herberg in 1955, "is the pervasiveness of religious self-identification along the tripartite scheme of Protestant, Catholic, Jew."[2] And the significance of one's religious identity extended beyond the religious realm. It influenced many aspects of a person's life—what neighborhood one lived in, what associations one joined, one's choice of marriage partner. According to Herberg, the close ties between religion and the American way of life made religious identity a form of national identity. "To be a Protestant, a Catholic, or a Jew are today the alternative ways of being American."[3] Forty years after this was written, Herberg's observation no longer holds in American society. Protestant, Catholic, and Jewish identities are no longer as closely linked to Americanness and, more importantly, the boundaries between these religious groups are no longer as defined as they once were.

The reasons for the declining significance of religious identity in American life are many. Due to the increased pluralism and secularism of public life, the Protestant establishment no longer holds an unchallenged position of authority. Furthermore, a resurgence of conservative Protestantism and the numerical growth of Catholicism, as well as an increase in the numbers of the religiously unaffiliated, have fundamentally altered the nature of religious relations in the United States. For example, there is a growing tolerance for a diversity of religious groups, revealed by increases in the rate of religious intermarriage. Moreover, from the mid-1960s to the present, there has also been a dramatic waning of denominational loyalty. People have become less concerned with denominational identity and subsequently are much more likely to change denominational membership in the course of their lives.

One of the main explanations behind this dilution of denominational loyalty—and the resulting attenuated social and political effects of denominational identity—is the decreasing difference in the social characteristics of the adherents of the different faiths. Catholics are now just as likely to attend college as Protestants. Meanwhile, as denominations have become less important for the religious life of the republic, parachurch organizations—independent organizations often drawing support from a broader interdenominational base on behalf of a particular political, social, or spiritual mission—have become more important. This is particularly true insofar as parachurch organizations provide the primary institutional framework within which an even broader and more portentous cultural realignment takes place.

Parachurch organizations now greatly outnumber denominations. They address a range of issues from evangelism to social service to politics. Their unprecedented growth, coupled with the weakening of denominational ties, has deepened century-old intrafaith divisions. How has this happened? These organizations tend to be partisan in nature and in agenda. More importantly, they also coalesce fairly tightly around the opposing ends of the cultural axis, defined at one end by a tendency towards orthodoxy and at the other by a tendency towards progressivism.

Thus, on the orthodox end of the continuum are organizations such as the Christian Coalition, Concerned Women for America, and the National Right to Life Committee, while the progressive end of the spectrum is represented by organizations such as People for the American Way, the National Organization for Women, and the National Abortion Rights Action League.

This division of special interest organizations according to their affinity with either progressive or orthodox understandings of moral authority highlights the fundamental transformation of religious relations today. The most significant religious divide in America is now across religious traditions rather than between them. In other words, orthodox Protestants share more in common culturally and morally with orthodox Catholics and orthodox Jews than they do with their fellow Protestants who are more progressive in orientation. Thus, in cultural and moral matters, one's position on the orthodox-progressivist continuum is more salient than one's religious identity per se. This change in the religious realm has profound implications for the society at large. It will impact how we as a nation answer such questions as: What kind of nation are we becoming? Are we for progress or for traditional values? And, what kind of future would we like to impart to the next generation? Before exploring in more detail the implications of this new religious divide for our public culture, we will discuss one fairly recent public incident that highlights the significance of the progressive-orthodox divide in public affairs.

THE CLARENCE THOMAS NOMINATION HEARINGS

At first glance, the controversy over Clarence Thomas's nomination to the Supreme Court might appear to have had more to do with racial and gender relations in this country than with religious divisions, especially given the nature of the charges put forward against Judge Thomas by law professor Anita Hill. While we are not arguing that racial and gender factors were unimportant to the conflict, we do insist that the Thomas-Hill confrontation conformed perfectly to the institutional dynamics of the culture war and the disagreements over moral authority that fuel such disputes. Interestingly, at the conclusion of Hill's testimony, Senator Biden wearily observed that Hill appeared to have been embroiled reluctantly in something over which she had no control. It is our contention that what occurred in the Senate confirmation hearings in 1991 was larger and beyond the control of all those involved—Judge

Thomas, Anita Hill, the Senate, the Judiciary Committee, and the White House. This confirmation battle was nothing less than a perfect illustration of the culture war over the meaning of America that is currently raging in various settings across the country.

The Thomas confirmation hearings divided Americans not so much by race and gender as by cultural affiliation. Women and the black community were sharply divided—and divided along cultural lines. William Galston, a political scientist from the University of Maryland and a former member of the White House staff, supported this interpretation of the polling data, by suggesting that the absence of a significant gender or racial gap during the hearings demonstrated the importance of cultural and class divisions "in determining the outcome of the struggle."[4] Thus, Clarence Thomas and Anita Hill became symbols of the opposing sides in the culture war, each invoked by special agenda organizations to bolster support for their differing ideals as to what America should be. Thomas, a conservative whose ideas drew from the Natural Law tradition of legal theory, was supported by at least 75 conservative special interest groups, including the National Association of Evangelicals, Concerned Women for America, and the Christian Coalition. In contrast, Hill was promoted as a symbol of the Democratic party's liberal agenda with over 50 progressive special agenda groups—including the Leadership Conference on Civil Rights; the National Association for the Advancement of Colored People (NAACP); the National Organization for Women; and the National Baptist Convention, USA (the nation's largest black organization)—supporting her claims.

In rebuttal to the accusations of Professor Hill, Clarence Thomas said that the eleventh hour hearing into ten-year-old charges of sexual harassment was "not what America is about." As we shall see, the very definition of "what America is about" is at the heart of the culture war— a war fought over competing (progressive and orthodox) moral visions of America, moral visions that have been institutionalized in the plethora of special agenda institutions already lined up on both sides of the cultural fault line.

COMPETING MORAL VISIONS

Today's realignment of American public culture takes institutional form in a shifting configuration of religious and political associations and organizations. At issue are two relatively distinct and competing perspectives on public life, which we identify as predominantly either "progressive" or "orthodox." Does it go too far to suggest that each side of the cultural divide represents something as coherent as a "perspective"? Certainly there are no comprehensive philosophical treatises that fully articulate the nature and profile of each side's competing moral visions. There are no manifestos declaring a coherent system of programs and goals for each side. What actually exists in the public discussion are, very often, nothing more than jumbled accumulations of pronouncements, accusations, appeals, and partisan analyses. It would be foolish to deny the complexity of the public debate, not to mention the intricacy and subtlety of the differing moral commitments in the hearts and minds of ordinary Americans. Americans locate themselves across a broad spectrum of values and perspectives. Yet, despite this complexity, it is possible to discern certain cultural tendencies. That is to say, all of these pronouncements, allegations, complaints, and appeals would seem to reveal broad, yet nevertheless distinct and opposing cultural impulses. These impulses suggest the existence of distinct, comprehensive visions of public life—public philosophies whose general contours we can roughly sketch as ideal-types.[5]

COMPETING PHILOSOPHIES OF AMERICAN PUBLIC LIFE

One of the chief tasks—and difficulties—of a public philosophy is the enunciation of national identity: deciding who we as a nation have been, coming to grips with who we are now, and defining what we shall become in the future. Often the mechanisms for articulating our public philosophies (and thus the meaning of our national identity) are nothing more than simple narratives—chronicles that begin with an account of our nation's mythic origin and conclude with a vision for our nation's future. The importance of these stories is critical. When they are intelligible, credible, and compelling, they not only inspire cohesion within communities, but they provide a ready justification for a nation's conduct in world affairs—for only that which is consistent with a nation's self-conception (what it has been and what it aspires to be) will be an appropriate field of national endeavor. What follows is an overview of two opposing public philosophies, that is, two competing understandings of freedom and justice in America today.

Freedom and Justice: The Orthodox Vision

The meaning of freedom emphasized within the orthodox tradition is the freedom enjoyed by a society when it does not live under despotism, the freedom of a society to govern itself or what the philosopher Charles Taylor has called "civic freedom."[6] It is precisely for this reason that the contrast between the United States (or the "free" world) and the former Soviet Union (and the Communist bloc) played such an important part in the evangelical and even the conservative Catholic worldview. Evangelicals and conservative Catholics operate with a definition of freedom that makes this contrast between freedom and oppression important.

The orthodox definition of freedom also highlights the importance of economic self-determination, as in the term "free enterprise." Notably, conservative Catholics have not championed this notion in part because of Rome's longstanding concern for the interests of organized labor. The book *The Spirit of Democratic Capitalism*, by Catholic scholar Michael Novak, is a notable exception to this rule. But, among the more vocal public theologians within the evangelical tradition, the celebration of capitalism—the freedom to pursue economic gain without governmental interference—is virtually unqualified.[7] Jerry Falwell has repeatedly claimed that "God is in favor of freedom, property, ownership, competition, diligence, work and acquisition. All of this is taught in the Word of God, in both the Old and New Testaments."[8] Elsewhere, Falwell has written that "the free-enterprise system is clearly outlined in the Book of Proverbs in the Bible."[9] In a similar vein, Pat Robertson has contended that while "communism and capitalism in their most extreme, secular manifestations are equally doomed to failure . . . free enterprise is the economic system most nearly meeting humanity's God-given need for freedom."[10]

Underlying these evangelicals' reverential endorsement of capitalism is the conviction that economic and spiritual freedoms go hand in hand, that one is impossible without the other.[11] As the economist (and professed evangelical) George Gilder put it: " 'Give and you'll be given unto' is the fundamental practical principle of the Christian life, and when there's no private property, you can't give it because you don't own it." For this reason, he concludes that "socialism is inherently hostile to Christianity and capitalism is the essential mode of human life that corresponds to religious truth."[12]

In the same way that orthodox traditions emphasize a particular understanding of freedom, so, too, do they emphasize a particular definition of "justice." Justice, by and large, is generally defined by the orthodox in terms of Judeo-Christian standards of moral righteousness. As R. J. Rushdoony makes clear, justice can only be understood in terms of the law, which in its highest form is "theocentric" and manifests "the nature and life of the ontological Trinity."[13] A just society, therefore, is a morally conscientious and lawful society. It is also an ordered society. The Old Testament dicta are often quoted in this regard: "righteousness exalts a nation," "by justice a king gives a country stability," "when the righteous thrive, the people rejoice; when the wicked rule, the people groan," and so on. According to this view, the moral fiber of American life is built upon standards of biblical morality. As a brochure from Christian Voice proclaimed, "the mandate from our Heavenly Father is to make sure government is faithfully meting out justice and punishing what is wrong and rewarding what is right."[14]

In this worldview, freedom, justice, and America's biblical culture are intimately linked to one another. Summarizes Tim LaHaye, "in truth, what has granted more freedom for the longest period of time . . . to the largest number of people, while at the same time producing the greatest wealth for the most people, can be traced to . . . our Bible-based form of government and our unique Bible-based educational system."[15]

This vision of America's past contains an implicit vision of America's destiny. In language reminiscent of nineteenth-century exceptionalism, a Students for America brochure announces that "America has a unique mission to extend the boundaries of liberty and righteousness."[16] But, from the conservative evangelical perspective, the only hope for achieving this end is for America to stay the course. If change is necessary, then it should be achieved in more perfectly fulfilling the ideals established at the nation's founding. So warns Pat Robertson, "either we will return to the moral integrity and original dreams of the founders of this nation . . . or we will give ourselves over more and more to hedonism, to all forms of destructive anti-social behavior, to political apathy, and ultimately to the forces of anarchy and disintegration that have throughout history gripped great empires and nations in their tragic and declining years."[17]

The Progressivist Vision

Within the progressivist vision, freedom and justice are understood in ways fundamentally different from those on the orthodox side of the cultural divide. Progressivists tend to define freedom largely in terms of the social and political rights of individuals. This is what philosophy professor Charles Taylor has called "liberal" freedom (as opposed to "civic" freedom). It is, as Taylor puts it, "freedom in the 'negative' sense, a condition in which the individual is granted immunity from interference by others in his life, either by state or church or by other individuals."[18] The logic is unambiguous. As one religiously-based women's rights newsletter stated simply, "being oppressed is the absence of choice."[19] It is in this light that one can understand the progressive tribute to "pluralism" and "diversity." As Norman Lear of the People for the American Way argued, "first and foremost among our shared values is a celebration of diversity and respect for the beliefs of others."[20]

Based on this affirmation, it is not surprising that the founding myths advanced in progressive circles tend to focus on the struggle of our forefathers to establish and preserve "pluralism and diversity." The names of Roger Williams, George Washington, John Adams, Tom Paine, James Madison, and Frederick Douglass are commonly invoked as champions of these principles. As a People for the American Way brochure maintained, "throughout our history, American men and women have fought hard to make this country a better place. They fought for fair representation. Open debate. A healthy respect for diverse public opinion. . . . Thus, America is the freest . . . nation on earth. A legacy left to us by the Founders of our country."[21]

Justice, on the other hand, is understood by progressivists in terms of equity and the ending of oppression in the social world. Whether in the case of women, blacks, Hispanics and other racial minorities, homosexuals and lesbians, Salvadorian refugees, the Nicaraguan government, Palestinians, the black majority in South Africa, or the poor and laboring classes, justice means greater equity and the elimination of repressive relationships. Political rights play a role in the equation, but almost invariably economics also becomes a part, perhaps the central part, of the equation. It is in this light that, for example, the progressive journal *Christianity and Crisis* described the "minimum wage" as a "minimum justice";[22] that the Religious Network for the Equality for Women identified support for the Equal Rights Amendment, a comprehensive jobs program, affirmative action, an earning sharing provision within Social Security, and so on, with "God's call for justice";[23] and that, in 1988, Peace with Justice organizers identified "people of color, women, children, the hungry, the poor, small farmers," and the like, all "victims of injustice."[24]

Clearly, then, within both the orthodox and the progressive public theologies, the words "freedom and justice" carry enormous symbolic importance. Each side explicitly links these words and their broader vision of the public order to either scriptural referents or other universal ethical standards. Thus, the meanings of these terms on either side of the cultural divide are almost precisely inverted. Where the orthodox tend to define freedom economically (as individual economic initiative) and justice socially (as righteous living), progressives tend to define freedom socially (as individual rights) and justice economically (as equity). These differences would account for the different meanings each side imputes to the American founders in their struggle to build the republic. Both biblical and enlightenment themes are present in the historical record. Yet in public discourse, each theme is accentuated by each of the opposing sides at the expense of the other. However true or false the resulting account may be, history tends to be reduced to ideology, a means by which the social and political interests on each side of the cultural divide are legitimated.

PUBLIC PHILOSOPHY AND NATIONAL PRIORITY:
SURVEY RESULTS

Anything but abstract and inconsequential, both the progressive and the orthodox philosophies of public life translate into practical standards for evaluating America's identity and priorities in the global order. This was amply demonstrated in the 1987 "Religion and Power" survey."[25] The survey found that Protestants, Catholics, and Jews on both ends of the new cultural axis generally agreed that America bore tremendous responsibility in world affairs. Virtually all were prone to agree that the United States is not "pretty much like other countries" but "has a special role to play in the world today."[26] So too, leaders of all faiths were strongly disposed to affirm that "the United States should aspire to remain a world power" and not "a neutral country like Switzerland or Sweden."[27] But orthodox and progressive factions sharply disagreed as to how the United States should carry out that responsibility. When asked "how much confidence do you have in the ability of the United States to deal wisely with present world problems?" progressives in all three faiths were at least twice as likely as their more orthodox counterparts to say "not very much" or "none at all."[28]

The same kind of division was exhibited among the orthodox and the progressive when asked to make moral assessments of America's place in the world order. The overwhelming majority of the orthodox in Protestant (78 percent), Catholic (73 percent) and Jewish (92 percent) leadership circles said, for example, that the United States was, in general "a force for good in the world." By contrast, the majority of the progressives in Protestant and Catholic leadership circles (51 percent and 56 percent respectively) said that the United States was either "neutral" or "a force for ill."[29] The contrast was even more stark when respondents were asked to assess how America treats people in the Third World. Progressives, particularly Protestants (71 percent) and Catholics (87 percent), were much more likely to agree that America "treats people in the Third World unfairly." The majority of the orthodox in each tradition claimed just the opposite.[30]

Opposing perspectives on America's moral status in world affairs became apparent when respondents were asked to compare the United States and the Soviet Union. A plurality of all religious leaders characterized the competition between the United States and the Soviet Union as a struggle in power politics, as opposed to a moral struggle. Even so, more orthodox Catholics and Protestants were three times more likely (and orthodox Jews over twice as likely) to say that it was a moral struggle.[31] Ideological disparities between orthodox and progressive were even more dramatic, however, when they were asked which was the greater problem in the world today: repressive regimes aligned with the United States or Soviet expansion? The majority of progressives within Protestantism (61 percent), Catholicism (71 percent), and Judaism (57 percent) claimed it was the repressive regimes aligned with the United States; the majority of the orthodox in these three faiths (Protestants, 84 percent; Catholics, 64 percent; and Jews, 87 percent) identified Soviet expansion as the greater problem.

The results of a survey of the political opinion of Christian theologians conducted in 1982 reveal similar divisions in perspectives on domestic spending.[32] Nearly two-thirds (63 percent) of the progressives compared to under one-fifth (19 percent) of the orthodox claimed that the government was spending too little on welfare. Eighty percent of the progressives said that the government was spending too little on national health compared to just 52 percent of the evangelicals. Likewise, nearly nine out of ten (89 percent) of the progressives agreed that the government was spending too little on protecting the environment; just half (50 percent) of the orthodox Protestants felt the same way. Almost nine out of ten (87 percent) of the progressives complained that the government spent too little money on urban problems compared to 56 percent of the orthodox. And roughly six out of every ten of the progressives (59 percent) claimed that too little was spent on foreign aid; just one out of every four (24 percent) of the orthodox agreed.

MORAL AUTHORITY AND THE REALIGNMENT OF PUBLIC CULTURE

Thus far, our main point has been simply to demonstrate that the orthodox and progressive each generally operate out of different and, in many cases, opposing visions of national identity and public life. Yet, even this does not quite capture what is fundamentally at issue here. To explain the nature of the emerging cultural realignment solely in terms of differences in public philosophy is to risk arguing that the primary contenders in the cultural conflict are really nothing more than "liberals" and "conservatives." The inadequacy of these words is immediately apparent. To conceptualize the problem as a squabble between religious liberals and conservatives or even political liberals and conservatives, as some have proposed, is to suggest that the new and opposing alliances in American public life operate on the same plane of moral discussion.[33] It suggests that each side shares the same commitments for national life, but that they simply envision different strategies for getting there. It is true that the orthodox tend to be conservative and the progressive tend to be liberal but those tendencies, we would contend, are merely the political manifestations of still deeper commitments. In reality, orthodox and progressive alliances do not operate on the same plane of moral discourse.

Others would argue that differences in political philosophy are reducible to social rank. The orthodox can be found among the disenfranchised lower middle class, the old petty bourgeoisie, who have incurred losses in power and privilege through the political and economic changes of the past decades. By contrast, this theory holds that progressives can be found among the rising "new class" of knowledge workers, the "new bourgeoisie," who have turned their control over cultural capital to social and political advantage. In its more vulgarized formulation, public philosophy is merely a reflection of class interests. What this perspective fails to see is that the "new class" of knowledge workers is divided within itself. Traditional family proponent James Dobson of Focus on the Family, for example, is every bit as much a knowledge worker or symbol specialist—and therefore a member of the new class—as is Patricia Ireland of the National Organization for Women.

Political formulations of the debate, then, would seem inadequate. Though there are clearly political manifestations of this dispute, the dispute is more than political. Likewise, while each side betrays certain social characteristics, the cultural controversy is much more than a reflection of competing class interests. There is, then, a more vital cultural dynamic involved in generating this cultural realignment. In this sense, the conflict is pre-political and pre-class. What ultimately explains the realignment in American public culture are allegiances to different formulations and sources of moral authority.

SOURCES OF MORAL AUTHORITY

To speak of moral authority is to speak of the fundamental assumptions that guide our perceptions of the world. These assumptions provide answers to questions about the nature of reality: what is real and what isn't. For example, is there a spiritual as well as a physical and material realm of existence? Does God exist? If so, what is God's nature? Is God an active agent in human affairs or a distant ideal of human aspiration? These are also the assumptions that define the foundations of knowledge—how we know what we know. Upon what do we ground our knowledge of the world, our understanding of truth, and our conception of moral and ethical behavior? Does this derive from divine revelation, through the analysis of empirical evidence, or through personal and subjective experience? These taken for granted assumptions act as a lens or a filter that highlights certain aspects of experience as important or unimportant, relevant or irrelevant, good or bad, and right or wrong. These generally unspoken assumptions provide the basic standards by which moral judgments and decisions are made.

It should go without saying (but the point needs to be made all the same) that all individuals ground their views of the world within some conception of moral authority. Not only those who are religious in a traditional sense but also those who claim to have no religious faith at all ground their views of the world in unprovable assumptions about "being" and "knowledge." To imagine otherwise would be philosophically naive. It is precisely for this reason that the Religious Coalition for Abortion Rights and the Religious Coalition for Equality for Women include in their fellowship such secularist organizations as the American Humanist Association and the Ethical Culture Society and speak of them literally as "communities of faith."[34] Even average, nonactivist secularists—ordinary people who maintain no religious belief, who worship no deity—hold and live by unspoken assumptions about their world; they, too, are people of particular, even if implicit, faith commitments.

Professor Richard Merelman has speculated that the strains in American culture exist between the "tight-bounded" and "loose-bounded" moral communities within American society.[35] Moral obligation within "tight-bounded" communities tends to be fixed and rigid, viewed by its members as a "given" of social life. Moral obligation in "loose-bounded" communities tends to be voluntary, contingent, and fluid—where the liberated individual, not the social group, becomes the final arbiter of moral judgment. Merelman's perspective does not contradict, but rather embellishes the argument made here. Namely, that what finally unites the orthodox and the progressive across tradition and divides the orthodox and progressive within tradition are different formulations of moral authority. Here again, the social reality is both complex and diverse. Even so, certain tendencies and commonalities exist on each side of the cultural divide that can be described in ideal-typical terms. What is the substance of each?

The Orthodox Appeal to Authority

Within the broader orthodox community, moral authority is rooted in a common commitment to transcendence, by which we mean a dynamic reality that is independent of, prior to, and more powerful than human experience. God and the realm God inhabits, for the orthodox, is indeed supernatural and supranatural. Of course, transcendence has a different content and meaning in each orthodox tradition. In each orthodox tradition, moreover, transcendence communicates its authority through different media: through the spiritual prerogatives of the inerrant Scriptures, both Old and New Testaments; through Torah and the community that upholds it; through the Pope and the traditional teachings of the Catholic Church; and through the Book of Mormon. Within each faith, the commitment to these specific media of moral authority is so forceful and unwavering that believers in each consider competing sources of moral authority as heretical.

Yet despite these differences, there are formal attributes to orthodox faith that are held in common. As argued earlier, each orthodox tradition maintains a paramount commitment to an external, definable, and transcendent source of authority. This is to say that for the believers in each tradition, moral and spiritual truths have a supernatural origin beyond but yet nevertheless graspable by human experience. Though the media through which transcendence speaks to people vary (as noted above), the orthodox all believe that these truths are divinely "revealed" and not somehow discovered through human endeavor or subjective experience. This implies that the orthodox also share a common method of interpreting their world and their experience. Transcendent authority is not just symbolic, but propositional; not just representational, but it has objective and concrete agency in human affairs. God, the orthodox would say, is real and makes himself tangibly, directly, and even propositionally known in the everyday experience of individuals and communities. From this authority derives a measure of value, purpose, goodness, and identity that is consistent, definable, and even absolute. In matters of moral judgment, the orthodox appeal unequivocally to these uncompromisable standards—standards that are universally valid, adequate in every circumstance and context for all time.

Based upon this general understanding of moral authority are certain non-negotiable moral truths. Among the most relevant for our discussion here are the assertions that the world and all of the life within it were created by God, and that human life, beginning at conception, is sacred. Another relevant orthodox moral truth is that the human species is differentiated into male and female not only according to genitalia, but also according to role, psyche, and spiritual calling. Related to this is the belief that the natural and divinely mandated sexual relationship among humans is between male and female and that this relationship is legitimate only under one social arrangement, marriage between one male and one female. Homosexuality, therefore, is a perversion of the natural and created order. This moral argument then becomes the foundation for the conviction that the nuclear family is the natural form of family structure and should remain inviolable from outside (state) interference. Subsequently, this reinforces the belief in the inviolable rights of parents to raise their children according to the parents' own religious and moral tradition—the implication being that this parental role should be encouraged and not hindered by a secular educational establishment.

The Progressivist Appeal to Authority

The progressivist vision of moral authority contrasts sharply with the orthodox. Progressivist moral authority is based, at least in part, in the resymbolization of historic faiths and philosophical traditions. Of course all religious communities (even the orthodox) resymbolize their traditions, but the orthodox tend to do so unwittingly and as a defensive measure when they feel threatened.[36] In the progressivist alliance, however, resymbolization is accomplished more or less consciously, deliberately, and in a way that is compatible with the spirit of historical change. Consider first the appeal to authority advocated by those who profess a progressive religious faith.

The premise of progressivist resymbolization more often than not is the intentional rejection of the form and content of orthodoxy. Such a rejection varies in degree and intensity, as one might imagine, but all progressives maintain to a certain degree that the language and programmatic thrust of traditional faith—at least as appropriated by their orthodox counterparts—is no longer relevant for modern times. Traditional faith must be reworked to conform to new circumstances and conditions; it must respond to new challenges and new needs. What compels this rejection of orthodoxy is the conviction that moral and spiritual truth is not a static and unchanging collection of scriptural facts and theological propositions, but a growing and incremental reality.

There is, therefore, according to the progressive worldview, no objective and final revelation coming directly from God. Scripture (of whatever form) is not revelation but only, and at best, a witness to revelation. The moral and spiritual truths of religious faith can only come to human beings indirectly and they can only be understood and expressed in human (which is to say, historical and institutional) terms. Thus, moral and spiritual truth can only be conditional and relative. For this reason, the legacy of faith for progressivists becomes valuable not as the literal account of historic personalities and events in relation to God, but primarily (and perhaps only) as a narrative pointing to ethical principles that can be applied to contemporary human experience. In the case of scriptural hermeneutics, what is important in the scriptural accounts of God's dealings with his people are not whether they literally occurred but what they symbolize about human relationships today.

In all of this there is a deep affinity between the cultural hermeneutics of progressive religious belief (Protestant, Catholic, or Jewish) and of civic (or a-religious) humanism. Both activist humanists (as found in such groups as the American Humanist Association, Ethical Culture, and the Council for Democratic and Secular Humanism) and the larger, nonactivist secularist public reject the validity of any traditional religious symbols and rituals. They also tend to hold a particular hostility toward orthodox religious belief.[37]

In sum, within the broader progressive alliance (both religious and secular), moral authority itself is rooted primarily if not exclusively within "this-worldly" considerations. The inner-worldly sources of moral authority may vary in at least two ways. First, the progressive conception can be based in what could be called, "self-grounded rational discourse." In intellectual terms, this is the tradition of "enlightenment naturalism"—a tradition of Thomas Hobbes, the Enlightenment encyclopedists, Baron D'Holbach, as well as of John Dewey, Willard van Orman Quine, Wilfrid Sellars, and the like.[38] Here, in principle, moral positions and influence are justified solely on the grounds of evidence about the human condition and the coherence and consistency of the arguments adduced. Not only are the nature of reality and the foundations of knowledge established by the adequacy of empirical proofs uncovered and the quality and coherence of the logic applied, but in this frame of reference, autonomous rationality and the empirical method become the decisive criteria for evaluating the credibility and usefulness of all moral claims as well. In the more extreme scientific formulations, the argument is made that there is no reality except that which science has shown to exist; no truth except that which is established by the scientific method. This is seen commonly in debates (often in the context of a lawsuit) over medical policy, educational policy, or other forms of public policy, where the ethics of a particular action—say in the area of genetic therapy, or in the value of educational curricula, or in the promotion of child care regulations—depend upon scientific proof that people are helped (or not hurt) by that course of action. If expert knowledge can show that a course of action has no untoward psychological effects on people, then that action is morally permissible.

On a second and very different plane of moral reasoning, the progressive conception of moral authority may be based in personal experience. This is probably the dominant basis of moral reasoning in progressivism. Once again, to put it in intellectual terms, this is the tradition of enlightenment subjectivism—of Kant, existentialism, and the various streams of Heideggerian hermeneutical philosophy such as is found in Wittgenstein and Richard Rorty. In this case, experience is ordered and moral judgments are made according to a logic that is rooted in subjective intuition and understanding. (The premise here is that by virtue of our symbolic activity, we human beings are responsible for the way the world is.) The moral logic of this position, as it translates into popular culture, has been described in numerous ways by social scientists in recent years—and sometimes derogatorily—as the "culture of narcissism," the "cult of the individual," "hedonism," "expressive individualism," the "self-fulfillment predicament," and so on. Each of these concepts implies a moral pragmatism centered around the individual's perception of his or her own emotional needs or psychological disposition. In this situation, reason linked with a keen awareness of subjective orientation provides the ultimate crucible for determining what is right and wrong, legitimate and illegitimate, and, ultimately, what is good and evil. In some ways, biography is the main foundation of truth.

As with orthodoxy, a list, if you will, of specific precepts tends to emanate from the progressivist conceptions of moral authority. Among the most relevant precepts for our present discussion is the assumption that personhood begins at, or close to, the moment of birth, at least until science can prove otherwise. Likewise, until science can prove otherwise, male and female are differentiated solely by biology; other differences are probably human constructions imposed upon biology through socialization and reinforced in human relationships by powerful and sometimes oppressive institutions. So, too, human sexuality is based in biological need. The forms in which those needs are met are historically and culturally variable and completely legitimate to the degree that those forms reflect a positive and caring relationship. Homosexuality, then, does not represent an absolute and fundamental perversion of nature but simply one way in which nature can evolve and be expressed. As one gay activist put it, we should "appropriate our sexuality not as something biologically necessitated, or as socially coerced, but as a freely chosen way of expressing our authentic humanness in relation to the special others with whom we wish to share our lives."[39]

In sum, orthodox communities order themselves, live by, and build on a shared commitment to transcendent truths and the moral traditions that uphold these truths. The very identity of these orthodox communities is "bound tightly" around that tradition.[40] In contrast, moral authority on the progressivist side of the cultural divide tends not to be burdened by the weight of either "natural law," religious prerogative, or traditional communal authority. Rather, as Merelman put it, it is a "loose-bounded" moral authority, detached from the cultural moorings of traditional group membership. It carries few if any of the burdens of the past. It has little memory to inhibit change. It is, in fact, distinctly forward-looking, open-ended, and malleable. This is a form of authority that is uniquely shaped by and oriented toward legitimating the prevailing Zeitgeist or spirit of the age.

Moral Authority and Political Expedience

Orthodox and progressivist conceptions of moral authority, and the range of specific assumptions that follow from these perceptions, are clearly more complex than we can depict in the rough sketches presented here. Nonetheless, what is important is that these orthodox and progressivist conceptions have a direct bearing on political philosophy and practice, including the most obvious controversial issues of the day: abortion, the Equal Rights Amendment (ERA), gay rights, educational policy, and the like. The interests and assumptions of each alliance—whether progressive or orthodox—preclude or endorse specific proposals from the outset and their moral logic reflects those interests and assumptions. Thus, for example, if human life is defined as beginning at conception, abortion is murder and must be stopped. If life is defined as beginning at birth or perhaps in the third or even in the second trimester of pregnancy, legalized abortion is morally acceptable and therefore a viable public policy. So, too, if it appears to threaten the "traditional" patriarchal family structure, equalizing the role of women will be undesirable. But, if the "bourgeois family" is regarded as just one of many possible familial arrangements (and one that tends in practice to be oppressive), legislation on behalf of the rights of women will seem both fitting and desirable. Similarly, direct correspondences between assumptions and policy positions can be found vis-à-vis debates over day care, eugenics, euthanasia, religion and public education, and a host of other issues.

But the relationship between moral authority and political expedience goes beyond predictable responses to policy issues. It is often asked how, for example, fundamentalist beliefs lead one to oppose America's relinquishing control over the Panama Canal, or how liberal Catholic beliefs lead one to support the proposition of "comparable worth." On the face of it, having certain religious commitments does not seem to have anything at all in common with certain specific political commitments; yet, seemingly strange patterns of alliance repeatedly surface in political life. Perhaps the best explanation for these patterns is simply that there is a loose affinity between religious orientation and political opinion. To be specific, there seems to be a loose affinity or "isomorphism" between religious conservatism and political preservationism, on the one hand, and between religious and even secular liberalism and political reformism (if not radicalism) on the other hand.[41]

Again, these general affinities lead people of particular cultural orientations to not-so-predictable political commitments. This would in part explain why, for example, the religiously orthodox tend to be more disposed toward a strong military and an aggressive foreign policy. The religious self-identity of orthodox groups tends very distinctly to draw from America's role as a world power (for example, by checking "godless'' Communist expansion or by defending Israel). Religious interests are at least indirectly tied to America's geopolitical interests. This isomorphism also partially explains the opposing relationships between religion and capitalism, particularly in Protestantism: the religious individualism of Evangelical Protestantism and economic individualism of capitalism mirror each other in much the same way that religious communalism (as expressed in the ethical tradition of the Social Gospel) and economic collectivism mirror each other. This would also explain why both orthodox and progressive camps (correctly) accuse each other of supporting policies that engender the intrusion of the state into private life. The enactment of law that endorses a shifting cultural climate will be perceived as an intrusion by those who resist the present cultural changes; the reversal of these laws or the attempt to prohibit their enactment will be perceived as an intrusion by those who approve of these changes and whose interests are served by them.

IN SEPARATE WORLDS

This overview has stressed the point that to label the alliances on each side of the cultural divide as liberal and conservative hardly does justice to the reality of the situation: it misses the central dynamic of the cultural realignment. What we have here are not just different positions on various issues, not just different public philosophies. These alliances, rather, reflect the institutionalization and politicization of two fundamentally different cultural systems. Each side operates from within its own constellation of values, interests, and assumptions. Each side has its relatively distinct conceptions of moral authority—two different ways of apprehending reality, of ordering experience, and of making moral judgments. Each side of the cultural divide, then, operates with a different moral vocabulary and moral semantic. Each side represents the tendencies of two separate and competing moral galaxies. The two sides are, indeed, ''worlds apart.''

As a consequence of this mutual moral estrangement, concessions on many policy matters become a virtual impossibility. The abortion debate exemplifies this most poignantly. No one on the pro-life side of the abortion controversy doubts that ''the gift of God's life begins at conception.''[42] How do we know this? For one, ''the Bible clearly states that life begins at conception.'' But what is more, modern science also demonstrates that there is life in the womb. (After all, ''the unborn child has a beating heart at 24 days, brain waves and unique fingerprints at

43 days, a complete skeleton and reflexes at 6 weeks," and so on.) "The abortion of the 22 million fetuses between 1973 and 1988," is therefore nothing short of "mass-genocide."[43] The moral choice, then, is clear: one is, as a Methodists for Life brochure put it, "either for life or against life; for Jesus or against Jesus."

The moral logic is fundamentally different on the pro-choice side of the controversy. Arguments also grounded in theological and scientific insight are constructed to show that there is "an important distinction between potential life and actual life" and that fetuses "are not of equal moral value with actual persons."[44] (After all, "the biblical character-ization of a human being is that of a complex, many-sided creature with the god-like ability and responsibility to make choices. The fetus hardly meets those characteristics."[45]) On this side too, as the Religious Coa-lition for Abortion Rights makes clear, abortion is a religious issue. The bottom line, according to RCAR and other progressive groups, is simply this: "If abortion is a religious issue, and religious theologies differ, and each denomination counsels its members according to its own theology, wouldn't a law prohibiting abortion violate religious liberty? Exactly. . . . The issue of abortion is a crucial test of religious liberty—one of the cornerstones of democracy."[46]

The reality of politics and public policy in a democracy is, for better or worse, compromise born out of public discussion and debate. But such discussion and debate would seem to be unattainable when the moral language employed by opposing sides is so completely antithetical. Whereas an Evangelical Protestant, charismatic Catholic, Hasidic Jew, or a Mormon might ask rhetorically: "How can murder be a First Amendment right?" A liberal Protestant, liberal Catholic, Reform Jew, or secularist might ask just the opposite: "How can the exercise of basic First Amendment rights be called murder?" Political resolution would seem sociologically impossible when the moral language for talking about mutual problems is so contrary. Virtually this same moral impasse has been reached in discussions about war, inequality, homosexuality, pornography and obscenity, euthanasia, and the use of fetal tissue for medical research. All of these disputes, as Alasdair MacIntyre has co-gently shown, are defined by their "interminable character."[47] True, not all of these issues are equally polarizing. Nevertheless, the existence of a common moral ground from which to build and resolve differences is elusive in every case.

What this means, among other things, is that orthodoxy and progres-sivism not only represent competing moral visions, but competing dogmas. This is true because what both sides bring to this public debate is, at least consciously, non-negotiable. What is ultimately at issue, then, are not just disagreements about "values" or "opinions." To use such language is to misconstrue the nature of moral commitment. Such language in the end reduces morality to preferences and cultural whim. What is ultimately at issue are deeply rooted and fundamentally different understandings of being and purpose.

To put this in the terms proposed by the French sociologist Emile Durkheim, what is ultimately at issue are different conceptions of the sacred. For Durkheim, the sacred was not necessarily embodied in a divine or supernatural being but was anything viewed as "set apart," "exalted," and "uncommon"—anything that provided the life-orienting principles of individuals and the larger community. To know the nature of the sacred in each moral community is to know the source of the community's passion, the root of its fervor. The reality, as Durkheim pointed out, is that communities cannot and will not tolerate the desecration of the sacred. The problem is this: not only does each side of the cultural divide operate with a different conception of the sacred, but the mere existence of the one side represents a desecration to the other.

Needless to say, this cultural realignment has tremendous historical significance. Few would disagree that the rise of Christianity as a world religion between the first and third centuries and the success of the Protestant Reformation in the sixteenth century provided the most fundamental divisions in the history of Western civilization—divisions between Christian and Jew and between Protestant and Catholic. The historical effect of these divisions was not only "religious" or cultural in nature but manifestly and irrefutably political in nature as well. These divisions have been at the root of centuries of prejudice and discrimination. They have been at the heart of social strife and even war.

But if the organizing principle of American pluralism is shifting in the direction described here—such that progressively-minded Protestants, Catholics, Jews, and secularists share more in common with each other culturally and politically than they do with the orthodox members of their own faith tradition (and vice versa)—then for all practical purposes, these two world-historical events have, at least in the American context, become both politically and culturally defunct.

If the organizing principle of American pluralism has shifted in these ways, then, it is because another world-historical "event" has become paramount. Yielding to the temptation of hyperbole, it could be said that the politically relevant divisions in the American context are no longer defined according to where one stands vis-à-vis Jesus or where one stands vis-à-vis Luther and Calvin, but where one stands vis-à-vis Rousseau, Voltaire, Diderot and Condorcet, and, in particular, their philosophical heirs (including Nietzsche and Rorty). It is, in other words, where one stands vis-à-vis the secular Enlightenment of the eighteenth century and its philosophical aftermath that fashions the divisions of contemporary public culture.

This, of course, is a caricature of our situation. Virtually everyone, nowadays, is influenced by the profound philosophical reorientation of the Enlightenment with its rejection of otherworldly "superstitions" and its emphasis on societal progress through human mastery and rational judgment. Even the most Bible-believing evangelical, the most Rome-bound Catholic, and the most observant Orthodox Jew has been influenced in subtle if unacknowledged ways. What really divides the culture is a matter of priority—the sources upon which different moral communities most rely in establishing their own sense of right and wrong. Clearly there are people at each extreme, particularly those people who act as the voices for opposing communities. But there are also many people somewhere in the middle, who draw in varying degrees from both Enlightenment and biblical sources of moral understanding.

Still, as a historical event, the Enlightenment has become an increasingly prominent source of division in American public life. The division is certainly both "religious" and cultural in nature, but it also has unmistakably political consequences. Already these divisions have begun to take expression as new forms of prejudice, discrimination, social strife, and political conflict.

NOTES

1. Portions of this chapter were originally published in chapter 4 of James Davison Hunter's *Culture Wars: The Struggle to Define America* (New York: Basic Books, 1991).

2. Will Herberg, *Protestant-Catholic-Jew* (Garden City, N.Y.: Doubleday Anchor, 1960), p. 256.

3. Ibid., p. 257.

4. "Thomas Hearings Resonate across U.S.," *The Washington Post*, 17 October 1991, p. A10.

5. One might just as well use the term "public theology" in this context. In the late 1960s, sociologist Robert Bellah coined the term "civil religion" to describe these general, quasi-religious visions of public life. For Bellah and

those who employed the term in the years to follow, however, civil religion meant something very specific. It was "the religion of the Republic," a vague if somewhat complex public myth whose symbolism was rooted explicitly in the biblical tradition—derivative of all biblical faiths but embodying none in particular—that served to legitimate national life. Few if any have come to doubt its existence, but many have debated whether it is a positive or a negative cultural force. For its proponents, it was a social glue that helped to bind the country together. For its critics, it was a tool cynically used in the rhetoric of politicians, a hollow ritual exhibited during times of national celebration and grieving, and an idolatrous form of religious nationalism that fundamentalists were particularly vulnerable to espouse. Either way, all of those who have used the term have maintained, at least implicitly, that nations (and America in particular) have just one civil religion. In truth, however, every religio-cultural tradition can and usually does construct its own mechanisms for legitimating national life. Our preference is to call these "public theologies." A complimentary view is offered by Robert Wuthnow, "Divided We Fall: America's Two Civil Religions," *Christian Century* 105 (20 April 1988): 395–99.

6. See Charles Taylor, "Religion in a Free Society," in *Articles of Faith; Articles of Peace: The First Amendment Religion Clauses and the American Public Philosophy*, J. D. Hunter and Os Guinness, eds. (Washington, D.C.: Brookings Institution, 1990), pp. 93–113.

7. This is not unique to today either. In 1945, the Reverend Carl MacIntyre wrote that "the Bible teaches private enterprise and the capitalistic system, not as a by-product or as some side line, but as the very foundation structure of society itself in which men are to live and render an account of themselves to God. . . . In the maintenance of the system of private enterprise is the life and liberty of the church itself." Carl MacIntyre, *The Rise of the Tyrant* (Collingswood, N.J.: Christian Beacon Press, 1945), pp. xiii, xv.

8. Jerry Falwell, *Wisdom for Living* (Wheaton, Ill.: Victor, 1982), pp. 102, 131. Likewise, the Christian Citizens Crusade holds that "the American system of private enterprise . . . was established . . . in accordance with the clear teachings of Scripture. Without it, our form of government, our way of life . . . could not exist" (from the Constitution and By-Laws of the Christian Citizens Crusade, Inc., Article IV, No. 5).

9. Jerry Falwell, *Listen America!* (New York: Doubleday, 1980), p. 13.

10. Pat Robertson, *The Secret Kingdom: A Promise of Hope and Freedom in a World of Turmoil* (Nashville: Thomas Nelson, 1982), pp. 151–52.

11. Nash makes precisely this argument in "The Christian Choice between Capitalism and Socialism," in *Liberation Theology*, Ronald Nash, ed. (Grand Rapids, Mich.: Baker Books, 1987).

12. Gilder is quoted in an interview from *Christianity Century* in Wuthnow, "Divided We Fall: America's Two Civil Religions."

13. R. J. Rushdoony, *Politics of Guilt and Pity* (Fairfax, Va.: Thoburn Press,

1978), p. 130. The entire chapter 5, "The Meaning of Justice," discusses this point.

14. From the pamphlet "Christian Voice: Preserving a Free Society," Christian Voice brochure.

15. Tim LaHaye, *The Battle for the Mind* (Old Tappan, N.J.: Fleming H. Revell, 1980), p. 37.

16. From the statement of principle in a Students for America brochure.

17. Pat Robertson, *America's Dates with Destiny* (Nashville: Thomas Nelson, 1986), p. 297.

18. See Taylor, "Religion in a Free Society," pp. 93–113.

19. This remark was made by bell hooks, who was quoted in *Common Ground—Different Planes: The Women of Color Partnership Program Newsletter*, April 1988.

20. Norman Lear, "The Search for Stable Values," in *Values, Pluralism and Public Education* (Washington, D.C.: People for the American Way, 1987), p. 42.

21. Brochure, People for the American Way, Washington, D.C.

22. Aaron Anderson and David Anderson, "A Minimum Wage for a Minimum Justice," *Christianity and Crisis* 48 (6 June 1988): 195–96. In a direct mail advertisement, *C & C* claimed: "Justice for the oppressed, and hope for the suffering. It's a simple message at the core of the Christian faith."

23. From a brochure/newsletter published by the Religious Network for Equality for Women sent to James Hunter in June 1988.

24. From the brochure announcing Peace with Justice Week, in 1988.

25. The survey part of the Religion and Power Project funded by the Lilly Endowment was conducted under the direction of James Hunter by the Opinion Research Corporation of Princeton, N.J. A sample of roughly 1,300 religious leaders was drawn from the 1985 edition of *Who's Who in Religion*. After deaths and nonforwarded mail were discounted, a total number of 791 individuals responded, representing a 61 percent response rate.

26. The question read, "Do you think the United States has a special role to play in the world today or is it pretty much like other countries?" Nine out of ten of the religious leaders in all categories chose the former, of the liberal Protestants, the ratio was eight out of ten.

27. The question read, "Do you think the United States should aspire to remain a world power or should it aspire to become a neutral country like Switzerland or Sweden?" Between 86 percent and 100 percent of all religious elites chose the former.

28. The actual figures of those saying "not very much" or "none at all" follow: Protestants: orthodox—21 percent, progressive—50 percent; Catholics: orthodox—25 percent, progressive—60 percent; Jews: orthodox—21 percent, progressive—45 percent. The chi square was significant at the .000 level.

29. The majority of liberal Jews (71 percent) also agreed that the United

States was "a force for good," but the gap between progressive and orthodox was still 21 percentage points.

30. The question actually read, "As a nation, do you think we treat people in the Third World fairly or unfairly?" The actual figures of those saying that America treats the Third World "unfairly" follow: Protestants: orthodox—27 percent, progressive—71 percent; Catholics: orthodox—50 percent, progressive—87 percent; Jews: orthodox—19 percent, progressive—39 percent. The chi square for this comparison was significant at the .000 level.

31. The question read, "How would you characterize the competition between the U.S. and the Soviet Union? Is it fundamentally a struggle in power politics or is it fundamentally a moral struggle?" The actual figures of those saying that it was a moral struggle, follow: Protestants: orthodox—43 percent, progressive—14 percent; Catholics: orthodox—39 percent, progressive—14 percent; Jews: orthodox—46 percent, progressive—21 percent. The chi square for this comparison was significant at the .000 level.

32. Catholics were included in this survey, but were not easily divisible into orthodox and progressive camps. For this reason, the results for evangelical and liberal Protestants are reported.

33. Robert Wuthnow conceptualizes the debate in this way in his book *The Restructuring of American Religion* (Princeton, N.J.: Princeton University Press, 1988).

34. References to this can be found in virtually all of the literature produced by these coalitions.

35. For an elaboration of these points, see Merelman, *Making Something of Ourselves: On Culture and Politics in the United States* (Los Angeles and Berkeley: University of California Press, 1984), p. 30. See also the essay by Robert N. Bellah, "Competing Visions of the Role of Religion in American Society," in *Uncivil Religion*, Robert N. Bellah and Frederick E. Greenspan, eds. (New York: Crossroad Books, 1987), p. 221.

36. Within orthodox Protestantism, see James Davison Hunter, *American Evangelicalism: Conservative Religion and the Quandary of Modernity* (New Brunswick, N.J.: Rutgers University Press, 1983). Within Orthodox Judaism, see Samuel Heilman, "The Many Faces of Orthodoxy, Part II," *Modern Judaism* 2, no. 2 (1982): 171–98.

37. Almost any issue of *Free Inquiry* and *The Humanist* reflects a particularly venomous opinion of orthodoxy, particularly of Evangelical Christianity. As to the general secularist public, the 1988 Williamsburg Charter Survey, "Religion and American Public Life," shows that the greatest popular hostility towards orthodoxy resides in this sector of the population.

38. See J. J. C. Smart, *Our Place in the Universe* (Oxford, England: Blackwell, 1989), for a cogent statement and summary of this view.

39. Rosemary Radford Reuther, in an essay in *Homosexuality in the Priesthood and the Religious Life*, Jeannine Gramic, ed. (New York: Crossroad Books,

1989); quoted in Richard John Neuhaus, "Homosexuality and the Churches," *First Things* 1 (May 1990): 68.

40. See the discussion of Merelman's concept of "tight-boundedness" in Robert Bellah, "Competing Visions of the Role of Religion."

41. Perhaps the best discussion of the concept of isomorphism is made by George Thomas, *Revivalism and Cultural Change* (Chicago: University of Chicago Press, 1989).

42. Jerry Falwell, *Listen America!*, p. 167.

43. From a brochure "Please Don't Pretend," published by the Christian Action Council, Washington, D.C.

44. This comes from a Religious Coalition for Abortion Rights brochure entitled "A Theological Response to Fundamentalism on the Abortion Issue," p. 9. As the author contends, "No one would deny the continuum of human development from fertilization to maturity and adulthood. That does not lead to the assumption, however, that every stage in the continuum merits the same value as 'life' or constitutes the same human entity."

45. Ibid., p. 11.

46. These quotations come from the Religious Coalition for Abortion Rights pamphlet entitled "Abortion: Why Religious Organizations in the United States Want to Keep It Legal." This is also the position of the Americans United for the Separation of Church and State, as articulated in a friend-of-the-Court brief filed with the Supreme Court in the famous *Webster v. Reproductive Health Services* case of 1989. Referring to the Missouri law's assertion that personhood begins at conception, the brief states, "such an inherently theological, but controversial, determination violates a core purpose of the establishment clause of the First Amendment—that is, the absolute prohibition against government preference of one religious sect or denomination over another and the placing of the state's imprimatur on a particular religious dogma." Reported in *Christian Century* 106, no. 14 (26 April 1989): 440.

47. Alasdair MacIntyre focuses on the issues of war, abortion, and justice/freedom. See his *After Virtue* (Notre Dame, Ind.: University of Notre Dame Press, 1984), pp. 6–8.

BIBLIOGRAPHY

Bellah, Robert N. "Competing Visions of the Role of Religion in American Society." In *Uncivil Religion*, edited by Robert N. Bellah and Frederick E. Greenspan. New York: Crossroad Books, 1987.

Heilman, Samuel. "The Many Faces of Orthodoxy." *Modern Judaism* 2, no. 1 (1982): 23–51.

———. "The Many Faces of Orthodoxy, Part II." *Modern Judaism* 2, no. 2 (1982): 171–98.

Hunter, James Davison. *American Evangelicalism: Conservative Religion and* the Quandary of Modernity. New Brunswick, N.J.: Rutgers University Press, 1983.

————. Evangelicalism: The Coming Generation. Chicago: University of Chicago Press, 1987.

————. Culture Wars: The Struggle to Define America. New York: Basic Books, 1991.

MacIntyre, Alasdair. After Virtue. Notre Dame, Ind.: University of Notre Dame Press, 1984.

Merelman, Richard. Making Something of Ourselves: On Culture and Politics in the United States. Los Angeles and Berkeley: University of California Press, 1984.

Nolan, James L., Jr., ed. The American Culture Wars. Charlottesville: University of Virginia Press, 1996.

Taylor, Charles. "Religion in a Free Society." In Articles of Faith; Articles of Peace: The First Amendment Religion Clauses and the American Public Philosophy, edited by J. D. Hunter and Os Guinness. Washington, D.C.: Brookings Institution, 1990.

Wuthnow, Robert. The Restructuring of American Religion. Princeton, N.J.: Princeton University Press, 1988.

III

Case Studies of Ethnic Conflict

4

The Tribes of Brooklyn: Race, Class, and Ethnicity in the Crown Heights Riots

Jonathan Rieder

Ever since a white driver back in 1991 hit and killed a seven-year-old black boy and a Brooklyn neighborhood exploded in violence, Crown Heights has joined Bensonhurst and Howard Beach as symbols of racial meanness in this often fractious polyglot city. The incident became one more of those ritual moments in which New York City periodically exorcises its racial demons. But the violence there, which included the murder of Yankel Rosenbaum by a raging black mob, had more than local significance. It was arguably among the very worst outbreaks of anti-Semitic violence in the United States. Beyond the compass of black-Jewish relations, the sorry episode resembles other moments in our national life—most obviously the Los Angeles riots—that proclaim the fragility of pluralism and the enduring power of tribalism. How to sort out its complexity thus remains an urgent necessity.[1]

For some observers trying to fathom those events, the narrative frame of racial conflict, no matter how disturbing, offered at least the reassuring compensation of familiarity. This was true despite the turn-around involved in the black attack on defenseless whites. Throughout the 1950s and much of the 1960s, the nature of the task of dismantling the racist system of segregation lent a certain clarity, both moral and cognitive, to the axis of white and black conflict. To some extent, moreover, the ambiguous legacy of the civil rights movement embedded in the still quite different fates of blacks and whites underscores the continuing vitality of racial categories. Much like the "first shall be last" chiliasm of the Nation of Islam, even the paradoxical, if no less chilling reversal contained in the narrative of black malevolence and white victims affirms that race still matters in the United States.

For others, Crown Heights offered about as pure a form of black anti-Semitism as one could find: how else to respond to the rampaging mob in hot pursuit of Rosenbaum and the cry of "Kill the Jew" it issued forth before it murdered him? As former New York mayor Ed Koch put it, "In Crown Heights over the last two weeks, there has not simply been displays of anti-Semitism, but a modern day pogrom. . . . Not since the last pogrom in Poland in 1946 has the Western world witnessed such an event."[2]

Surely, both anti-Semitism and black-white antagonism help make sense of various aspects of the conflict, and we shall have occasions to take heed of their power. Yet in a changing America, categories like black and white and black and Jewish no longer possess the force and clarity they once enjoyed. Part of this murkiness inheres in the ambiguities that surround decoding the meaning of racial and ethnic epithets, especially by outside observers who may not understand the communicative routines and linguistic codes that shape both the usage and significance of vernacular denigration. Thus, the meaning of "Hymie" or "schvartze" or even "Hitler should have finished the job" is not as precisely self-evident as one might assume. Some of this opacity is of relatively recent vintage; but some of it is timeless, too.

For example, in a gust of Anglophilia, an African-American gang that in the 1960s surrounded a white British professor at the University of Chicago met his bristling insistence that he was from England with an apology: "We thought you were a white guy." Similarly, among white working-class youths, the phrase "nigger," as indecent as the brutal associations of the word may be to the broader enlightened society, can signify various things depending on the context. It can mean "all black people." Or it can conjure up the particular black enemies uppermost in their mind at the time. "We only bother with the [black] ones that are like friends with us," a white ethnic high school student once told me. "But then there's always them fucking arrogant ones that . . . if you don't kill them, they'll kill you."

The volatility of group categories in contemporary America draws power as well from more structural realities, of which the interpretive ambiguities are, to an important extent, a response. New immigration, the rapidly changing nature of group discord, and class divisions within the black community all make race an increasingly elusive, even fading line of demarcation.

A moment's reflection on some of the anomalies in our group life highlights the instability of the present reality and the declining power of once familiar categories to make sense of it. A number of years ago, Korean Americans at Columbia College, rejecting membership in the broader communal rubric—and organization—of people of color, embraced the neologism ''Kew,'' signaling their identification with a Jewish strategy of mobility and identity. Meanwhile, in his 1992 Republican Convention speech, America-Firster Pat Buchanan apotheosized the immigrant shopkeepers of Koreatown and the automatic weaponry they used to stand down rioters. In New York City, there have been instances in which white employers, unenthusiastic about low-skilled ''black'' workers, flipped the workforce of their factories from African American to Afro-Caribbean, perhaps actually ''darkening'' the literal complexion of their employees. In the so-called ''black'' rebellion of the Los Angeles riots, Salvadorans and Mexicans took to the streets, and Latinos comprised the largest percentage of those arrested.

Such complexities, in which the swirling presence of elements of class, ethnicity, race, immigrant status, and generation defy neat and easy categorization, were no less evident in Crown Heights. The driver of the car that hit little Gavin Cato was not just white, or even just Jewish, but a Hasidic Jew from the Lubavitcher sect. Within that Hasidic community, there was much grumbling, and even downright anger, when the establishment Jewish organizations, perhaps some believed betraying a stance of moral superiority and emotional distance, did not immediately rush in to defend their less assimilated brethren. The victim was not simply an abstract black, but the son of Guyanese immigrants. Although African-American militants tried to cajole the Caribbeans with visions of black power, the ethnic divisions between them remained vivid. If the Crown Heights episode had elements of a fight between the races and war against the Jews, it also had elements of an ethnic punch-out between Hasidim and blacks that tells us much about the persistent tensions between tribalism and pluralism in contemporary American society. In the remainder of this chapter, I shall explore the basic outlines of the events of 1991 in order to highlight these ambiguous elements of tribalism at work.

Ironically, in defiance of the flamboyant nastiness that was the foundation of media depictions of the community, in more prosaic moments Crown Heights would seem to vindicate the idea of democratic mixing. On many of its tree-lined streets of modest brownstone houses and low-lying apartment buildings, blacks and Jews live commingled. The population of roughly 150,000, sandwiched between Bedford Stuyvesant, Prospect Park, Brownsville, and Flatbush, includes almost 90,000 Caribbeans (about half Jamaican, followed by Haitians, with many Trinidadians, Bajuns, and Guyanese), 35,000 Lubavitcher Jews, and a good sampling of African Americans. For a young Alfred Kazin, as he remembers in *A Walker in the City*, peering out of the ghetto of Brownsville, Eastern Parkway was where the Jewish "alrightnicks" lived. To aspiring West Indians in the 1950s, "ditchy" Crown Heights was the ultimate in upward mobility. Notwithstanding the toll of crack and Jamaican drug posses and the presence of many poor and marginally working-class blacks, the black residents are mainly working people of middling income, with many middle-class home owners, civil servants, and professionals. The Jews are also largely of middle income, including many teachers in public and Jewish schools, with some affluent and a sizable portion of poor among them as well.

The tensions that had been seething for two decades between Lubavitchers and blacks exploded on August 19, 1991, into an anti-Semitic rampage. The Lubavitchers, whose numbers include many Holocaust survivors, relived a painful history. "We had hoped that pogroms would remain only in history books," Rabbi Shmuel Butman insisted to me at the time. "We in Crown Heights saw a pogrom with our own eyes. This is not Poland in 1881. It's the United States in 1991!" In front of the main Yeshiva on Eastern Parkway, a mob of blacks chanted "Seig Heil" and "Hitler should have finished the job." Relying on mezuzahs and a black preteen informer, black mobs searched out and attacked Jewish homes. As a black mob pounded the car with rocks and concrete, and shards of glass flew through the air, a Lubavitcher yelled to the driver, "Run them over, kill them!" He recalled later, "Those animals were going to kill us. I didn't do anything to them!" The black mob chasing down Yankel Rosenbaum cried, "Kill the Jew"; the man accused of thrusting the knife had a grudge against his Jewish landlord and recently had retaliated with swastika graffiti in the building's lobby. Not long after the riots, on Rosh Hashanah, a bullet whizzed through a synagogue window.

Weeks after the incident, a state of terrorism prevailed near the Cato home, as a shadowy squad of vigilantes sought to effect its own version of ethnic cleansing. A Lubavitcher man active on the block related how a black man put his face into a baby carriage and menaced the Jewish mother, "We're going to burn you Jews out of here if you don't get out. Leave now." The Lubavitcher himself was accosted by a man who screamed, "I'm going to get my gun and shoot one of you motherfucking Jews. I'm going to put a bullet through those glasses on your head." When they awoke to find a swastika on the door with the warning "Leave Now," a Jewish family in the Cato building packed their bags.

The anti-Semitic thuggery left the Jewish community alone and wounded. Under such circumstances, the disproportion between the brutal realities of the streets and the ethereal efforts of the sponsors of black-Jewish dialogue could appear demonically perverse. One incensed Lubavitcher put it this way, "I can't trust people who aren't Jewish to stand up for me. And now I am supposed to go explain myself to people who don't like me because I am different. Fuck you! We're supposed to be different. If you want to understand me, read the Bible. I should explain my Succoth to you so you won't kill me!" Another Jewish man who had always admired the moral courage of blacks could not fathom the silence of black leaders. "What has happened to black people? Why will nobody condemn these black Nazis, the black Ku Klux Klan?"

This temptation to press the wild events into familiar narrative frames was natural enough. Perhaps it was irresistible, especially for the many Holocaust survivors who reside among the Lubavitchers. Clearly, more than a projective reading of history or some putative affliction of "Jewish paranoia" gave rise to the cries of "Pogrom," as the authorities proved unable, or perhaps, as some put it, unwilling to move decisively against the rioters and restore order. The Lubavitcher conviction that Mayor David Dinkins intentionally held back the police force reinforced this sense of "the abandonment of the Jews," and it would later become the fulcrum of a lawsuit against Dinkins and the city. An editorial in *The Jewish Press*, a voice of Jewish Orthodoxy, asked, "Can anyone in Crown Heights feel safe again with a mayor who leans over backwards not to confront the black hoodlums who are running this city?"

The resonant metaphors of pogrom and Kristallnacht captured undeniable aspects of the conflict, especially as many Jewish residents themselves felt the terror. They evoke timeless aspects of Jewish experience, above all the primal sense of physical vulnerability created by unchecked thuggery. Such immemorial anxieties about safety were reinforced by the failure of the state to protect the residents of Crown Heights from "Cossack" hooligans. Finally, street-level activists with reputations for attitudes inimical to Jewish interests and sensibilities, as well as in some cases for explicit anti-Semitism, entered the scene and inflamed the local situation.

And yet these considerations ignore all the countless features of the Crown Heights situation that did not fall neatly into the narrative of black-Jewish conflict or black-white conflict. First, there was hardly a unified ''black'' community engaged in ''war against the Jews.'' Second, the actual meaning of the mob's anti-Jewish rhetoric is hardly self-evident. Finally, the violent rampage of blacks against the Jews was a specialized current within the broader context of black-Jewish relations in Crown Heights.

Perhaps the most distinctive, and portentous feature of the anti-Semitism of the mob was its yoking to the violent rage of a certain constituency of young, less privileged blacks. That retributive passion is no simple unalloyed force. A compound of class resentment, racial outrage, and plain wilding, it is a molten force that in recent history has flowed against Jews, the police, white people in general, Korean grocers, a white woman jogging in Central Park, reporters, black reporters, homeless people, and other blacks more generally. The same pattern of lower-class male dispute-settlement, with its repertoire of violent reprisals, collective allocation of blame, and communal vengeance, appear just as regularly in black-on-black gang violence.

Moreover, despite the alarming rhetoric of ethnic denigration, there was little evidence of coherent, formal anti-Semitic belief systems at work in Crown Heights. For the provincial whose knowledge of Jews is confined to the Hasidim nearby, ''Jew'' can be a way of marking people vividly different from them and ''Seig Heil,'' unlike when uttered by skinhead ideologues, a way to get even with local tribal opponents. Also, ''Jew'' for some denotes the most immediate incarnation of white people; one agitator cursed ''the Jew Caucasians.'' When a mob spotted reporter Jimmy Breslin in a taxi, the cry went up, ''White man. White man.'' They dragged him out, stripped and beat him. Breslin's black rescuer explained, ''It isn't just you. They don't like white people.'' After a grand jury failed to indict the Jewish driver who'd killed Gavin Cato, the sound of reggae blared on President Street: ''Murder them. Murder them. Hunt down all the white men and murder them.'' To some extent, then, we are dealing with an ethnically resonant variant of a more general phenomenon of alienation, antiwhite resentment, and retributive frustration that courses through certain, mainly economically marginal regions of black life.

Other youths yielded to a Dionysian frenzy, looting stores owned by Jews, an Iranian, and Koreans, scooping up the goods at the Sneaker King and the Gold Exchange. Nor was the frenzy of the hoodlum element who seized the streets utterly without political content. At the time, some voiced their indignation over what they took to be a pattern of injustice in the police refusal to arrest the driver who had run over the boy, recent attacks by whites on black residents in the Brooklyn neighborhood of Canarsie, and the innocent verdict in a rape case at St. John's College, in which white defendants allegedly sexually abused a Jamaican student. The mob chasing Rosenbaum chanted the activist mantra, "No Justice, No Peace."

African-American youths from the projects were highly visible in the rioting, and, after the first night, many streamed into Crown Heights from outside the community. But a striking feature was the participation of at least some Caribbean youths. According to local blacks, Jamaican youths predominated among the Caribbeans. In a perceptive piece in the *Village Voice*, Peter Noel caught that Jamaican presence in the eye of the mob: "We ah go bu'n (burn) dem devils, Rasta. We want justice. We nah want nonna dem marching bizness. Way yu ah say? Night time ah de right time. We ah fe dead fe justice! Dead."[3]

This involvement marks a generational chasm that may expand the market for resentment politics among the least privileged sectors of the Caribbean population, a pattern evident as well among second- and third-generation Mexican gangs in California. Traditionally, many striving West Indians, once dubbed "black Jews," have associated "blacks," their denigrative term for American blacks, with criminality and shiftlessness. They worry that the values of the streets will capture their kids. As Phillip Kasinitz, author of *Caribbean New York*, observes, the least successful Caribbeans are prone to assimilate not with the broader society, but with the black underclass that repudiates it. "Many Caribbean parents are shocked at what their children are becoming—or as they see it—what being black has done to their children. 'You're becoming American,' is how disapproving parents scold their kids."

Moreover, some second- and third-generation West Indian youths, as well as African-American ghetto kids, imitate the Johnny-too-bad style of the Jamaican drug posses, dreadlocks and all. The Badass of gangster rap and the Rude Boy of reggae both embody an ethos of defiant masculinity at odds with former Mayor Dinkins's aura of decorous respectability. When Dinkins went to the Cato family's house, his plea for peace was met with a fusillade of bottles, and the crowd screamed "Traitor"

and ''The mayor's not safe.'' Such tensions mark lines of cleavage—
partially but not completely coinciding with class—within the ''black''
communities, both African-American and West Indian, between vulgar
and genteel, alienated and more trustful, segments of the community.

As they did during a boycott of Korean grocers in nearby Flatbush
one year previously, African-American separatists sought to capitalize
on Caribbean anger. A statement from Sonny Carson, a nationalist activist, addressed the youthful warriors who had smashed Jewish windows
and heads: ''White America and Black Uncle Toms call you Hoodlums.
. . . We call you the children of Malcolm X.'' Underneath a picture of
black youth smashing a huge wooden pole through a police car wind-
shield ran the exhortation to ''The Heroes of Crown Heights Rebellion''
to remember Soweto and Palestine. This political psychodrama was the
nationalists' identity-boosting version of ''You are somebody.'' *Boyz n
the Hood* had become the Intafada.

Even at this relatively ''elite'' level, among grassroots activists the
category of Jewish opponent lacked clarity and consistency. In the vol-
atile rhetoric of the demagogues, the Jews kept dissolving into generic
whites, betraying the significantly derivative quality of the anti-Semitism.
The street orators worked to enfold the Caribbeans in a larger community
of black affliction, bound together by the racist enemy. During the Howard Beach attack, in which a white racist pack attacked a group of black
men and chased one of them, Michael Griffith, out onto a highway where
he was killed by a speeding car, this made sense: the white mob did not
discriminate between their West Indian victims and American blacks.
But the Crown Heights affair involved an accident. In truth, the moral
equivalence was between Yankel Rosenbaum and Yusuf Hawkins (another black man attacked by a white racist mob), both killed by racial
hatred. Dinkins made the equation; decrying particularistic notions of
racial purity, he affirmed the moral community of universalism, branding
the racial murder of Rosenbaum a ''lynching.'' But that sharing of a
metaphor of the black experience scrambled the boundaries of the community. Black nationalist Elombe Brath, fuming at Dinkins's empathetic
linking of the two, restored purity with the distinction between retaliation
(Rosenbaum) and premeditation (Hawkins). ''His comments are the most
insane and insulting of all. The mayor does not seem to distinguish
premeditated murder from retaliatory murder.''[4]

A simple emotional economy underlay Brath's abhorrence of mixing:
sympathy was reserved for those within ''the family,'' the phrase that
often appears in preachments to ''buy black'' and ''keep it in the fam-

ily." There were brother people and other people, Africans and devils, sun people and ice people. Once again, we confront the recurrent tendency of anti-Semitism to collapse into the broader rubric of antiwhite sentiment, itself a response to the perception of pervasive black suffering and white racism.

The imagery of the family's vulnerable youth helped transmute an accident into racist intentionality. Speaking at the Cato funeral, Reverend Al Sharpton placed little Gavin in the Afrocentric family formed by the line of blacks destroyed by white malevolence—making the Guyanese boy kin not just to the martyrs of the outer boroughs, Yusuf Hawkins and Michael Griffith, but, even more primally, to the Scottsboro boys, those iconic victims of Southern lynching, and the four girls blown up in a Birmingham, Alabama, church. The brute realities of class and the weapons of black drug dealers endanger black children more immediately than do Hasidic drivers and Eurocentric curricula. But the formulations of "Our children are dying" and "We are killing our children" were rejected in favor of, to quote Sonny Carson on Gavin Cato's death, "They"—meaning the crackers, or whites in general—"are killing our children." Dinkins sat alone in the church, but in a show of racial solidarity, Sharpton included him in the family: "These people don't like you no better than they like us." Sonny Carson outdid everyone, loonily invoking an infamous case of cannibalism in Milwaukee: "Now, they're eating us."

For all the rhetorical efforts of the activists, the diversity of opinions among Brooklyn "blacks" defied the effort to bind them into a vast black community. The rioters, complained a Barbadian woman, had besmirched the ethnic honor of West Indians. In one of those folk conversations that takes on broader ritual significance in times of crisis, an argument on a Brooklyn subway train evoked the rival interpretive positions at war in the "black" community. A Jamaican woman railed that Jews had murdered a black boy and white police had refused to arrest him. A Saint Vincentian woman who told me about the incident, replied, "It was an accident. It wasn't murder. There's a difference." The African-American woman sympathized. Her son had been killed by a car driven by a black man, who hadn't been indicted either: she had wanted revenge, but she came to understand that this is the law. The riled Jamaican woman, her patois becoming thicker, insisted that this was just what whites did to blacks in Jamaica a long time ago. This subway incident was a fight not about facts but about preferred narratives: how to construe history, how to explain affliction, how long to hold a grudge.

The divisions that were emerging across the borough of Brooklyn and New York City were no less evident in Crown Heights itself. The neighborhood was not totally marked by black-Jewish recrimination. Before the accident, wary blacks and insular Hasids found time for moments of tolerance, even of camaraderie. Gavin Cato played with Jewish children on his block. Two years earlier, a black driver without license, registration, or insurance had run over and killed a three-year-old Hasidic child. "Did the Jewish community put 150 cops in the hospital?" Rabbi Butman asked me, "Did Jews put a bullet through a church? Did we vandalize African-American homes?" Another Lubavitcher recalled, "The man was shaken, so the Jews brought him coffee. They acted like menschen." After the riots following the Gavin Cato killing, some black residents seemed to take pains to nod, as if declaring, "that wasn't me," and black neighbors spoke of their anger that hoodlums from outside the community made a fuss over an accident. A Haitian cabby with Jewish friends empathized with Lubavitcher nervousness: "As I get close, I can tell, the Jews are thinking, 'What's he going to do to me? Is he one of the guys who broke my windows?' "

Despite the efforts of the African-American activists to build a Caribbean clientele and to construct a community around the purity of color, they confronted obstacles that made the achievement of pan-African unity difficult. Early on, there were rumbles of resentment over the African-American putsch of a West Indian community. The angriest Jamaican youths were not quite ready to line up behind the American activists. Nor did mainstream Caribbean leaders rejoice at their presence. Carson's lame effort to unfurl the Guyanese flag at Gavin Cato's funeral, a pan-Africanist version of eating bagels and cannoli on election day, signaled the activists' predicament.

The approach of the West Indian-American Day Parade revealed the chasm between the African-American activists and their immigrant colleagues (and mainstream African-American leadership). In the end, Caribbeans opted for a vast outpouring of carnival release. Sonny Carson repudiated the two million people who turned out for the parade: "It was a shame before God that people had the audacity to party . . . where the [Cato] boy was killed." The Caribbean community struck back hard in the *Carib News*. Where did African-American activists get the nerve "to tell the Caribbean community . . . how best to conduct struggles for justice." Leader after leader affirmed the healing of Hasidic-black dialogue, as well as the warm welcome Hasidic rabbis received from black Brooklyn leaders, West Indian and African-American alike, during the parade. Roy Hastick, president of the Caribbean-American Chamber of Commerce and Industry, decried Reverend Herbert Daughtry's reported critique of "grinning and skinning on Eastern Parkway" as disrespecting Caribbean people. Caribbean people are not, he insisted, "a party people. . . . We do not just 'grin and skin' . . . we are a serious people."[5]

These divisions among and within various segments of the "black" community once again mark the fluid, shifting, and contingent nature of the identities engaged by the struggle and the limits of seeing the conflict only in black-white or black-Jewish terms. But neither does this offer sanguine evidence of a harmonious mosaic. If the Caribbean leadership mainly disavows the politics of racial resentment, this does not mean that ethnic politics never get nasty. New York City is full of tribal animosity: Italians against blacks, Satmar Hasidim against Lubavitcher Hasidim, Haitians against Koreans. In Harlem, African Americans and Latinos were recently locked in fierce struggle over plans to open a Pathmark supermarket. During the Crown Heights violence, West Indians blamed the rioting on American black hoodlums. Barbadians would tell you, "the Jamaicans did it." The Orthodox Jews who used to read Meir Kahane's fulminations in the nationalistic *The Jewish Press* shared his tribal recoil from "Hellenized" Jews on the Upper West Side. In Williamsburg, Brooklyn, the explosive struggle features Hasidim from the Satmar sect against Hispanics. Lest we rush to seize this as evidence of an unprecedented "Balkanization" and "fragmentation" of America, we would do well to remember the longstanding pattern of ethnic, religious, and racial rivalry that has punctuated American history.

Placed in these larger macrocontexts, it is not strange that the black and Lubavitcher tribes of Crown Heights have been sparring for decades over power, real estate, respect, and alternate-side parking spaces. Black-Lubavitcher tensions in this area must be understood in terms of these real conflicts, as well as of the explosive class-based tensions that spurred the violence on the streets. Indeed, the violence was a specialized current, carried out by an equally specialized sector of the community within the totality of ethnic relations in Crown Heights.

Lubavitchers rightly bristled at the idea of "legitimate complaints"; as an apology for anti-Semitic violence, it is obscene. Were there two sides to Auschwitz, a Lubavitcher demanded of me? Didn't Himmler have grievances? Yet, even if such "reasons" neither explain nor justify the violent rioting, they do help explain the plaints of Jewish arrogance and special treatment that long have been voiced by dignified Caribbean pluralists who held no truck with Sonny Carson and the rude boys.

The history of this larger pattern of communal strife originated in a weird version of ethnic succession. The pious Hasidim—Jews not enamored of enlightenment pieties and mixing with the gentiles—found themselves in their earthly predicament because they did not run from racial transition. In the 1960s, as pressure on Crown Heights from blacks intensified, panic-plying blockbusters worked to stampede whites. Many of the Lubavitchers' less observant Jewish comrades, including many Hasidim of different sects, fled southward to places like Canarsie or jumped to "The Island" (Long Island). But Rebbe Schneerson told his flock to stay, and they did.

Law and order, pro-life Republicans nationally, religious triumphalists unimpressed by the refinements of civil religion, the Lubavitchers were hardly prime candidates for this mission. More observant Jews tend not to prize integration—with anybody, but especially with blacks. Even without their fierce spiritual identity, which bequeathed the requisite urban stamina, fear of black crime would have produced a certain huddling together. Over the decades, the Orthodox community in Crown Heights has been the victim of brutal street crime, and the culprits have usually been blacks. In one famous case, two black robbers, enraged at getting no booty, killed a Holocaust survivor who was traveling without money in deference to Sabbath requirements.

The Lubavitchers responded to danger in a geopolitical fashion: with patrols and border guards. That these pallid Torah-lovers could intimidate black and Hispanic muggers may strain credulity. But when it comes to Jewish survival, such partisans of Judeocentricity were not restrained by liberal squeamishness. A non-Hasidic Orthodox Jew I once interviewed after he left Crown Heights remembered, "We had vigilantes in Crown Heights, and we stopped the niggers there!" Imagine you are a Williamsburg Latino, out for a stroll. As you approach a Hasidic block, the shriek of whistles summons scores of bearded men dressed in black hats who tweet until you reach the next block, and its whistleblowers begin their shrieking. In Crown Heights, as in Williamsburg, the Hasid crime patrols have often administered justice themselves rather than trusting to New York courts. Local blacks have sometimes exulted when Lubavitcher patrols beat a car thief or a mugger, and over the years there have been efforts at joint black and Jewish patrols. But the Lubavitchers' vigorous questioning of blacks they deem out of place, as when they physically detained a black youth merely because he was racing for the subway, has rankled many as racist presumption.

Black reaction was intense when Lubavitchers, following an unrelated police killing of a black businessman, beat a black man to a pulp—he later died—after he allegedly grabbed a man's yarmulke. The trial strategy of the Hasids did not reassure the community that Jews were a justice-loving people who valued race-neutral procedures over tribalism: they surrounded the defendants with other Jews in black hats and beards. The witnesses could not, as they say, "tell them apart." It was this incident that spurred the first black mobilization against the Lubavitchers, the United Black Front.

The ability of the Hasidim to organize crime patrols reflects the communal power that flows from their cohesiveness, centralized structure, and bloc voting. Divested of their cabalistic edge, black complaints over the years of special Jewish privilege have been more than projective fantasy. In the past, mayoral candidates, New York's governor Mario Cuomo, and international politicians came to pay their respects to Rabbi Schneerson. To concentrate Jewish power, the Lubavitchers fought to place the Bedford Stuyvesant portion of the old Crown Heights north of Eastern Parkway beyond the borders of the current district. And in countless other ways, they used the political process to acquire public resources, from funds for poor Jews (much to the chagrin of black homeowners, they sought to have the district labeled a poverty area) to acquiring city-owned properties for renovation.

Blacks also charged that police show undue deference to the Lubavitchers when they violate parking regulations on Jewish holidays. They said police "pamper" Lubavitchers by letting them rope off Kingston Street on the Sabbath, restricting black access to their homes and businesses. For years before the accident, the Grand Rebbe's police guard was a lightning rod for resentment of Jewish "special treatment."

Given that Hasidic power had been in decline at the time of the accident, is it possible still to argue that these plaints about Jewish hegemony were not the distortions of resentment and paranoia? We should be careful of dismissing the rationality of the grievances too quickly. As cognitive psychologists, rational choice theorists, and economists have long stressed, rationality comes in many forms and rarely attains perfection. No less than their white neighbors, blacks scan the environment, estimate influence, and assess fairness within the confines of the information available, the flamboyant if unrepresentative signs and incidents that serve as ad hoc measures of reality, and their own distinctive perspective.

As a result, viewed suspiciously by blacks primed to be suspicious by local history and by more general skepticism about the good faith of whites and the possibility of fair treatment, the murky particulars of the Cato accident, especially as distorted by demagogues, could reasonably trigger black indignation. The ambiguity of when the Jewish and public ambulances arrived and left gave full play to black mistrust. Did the Jewish ambulance rescue the Jewish driver instead of ministering to Gavin Cato pinned under the car? Did Schneerson's motorcade habitually go through red lights? If one were not schooled in New York law on vehicular manslaughter but believed the police favored Lubavitchers in countless ways, the failure to arrest and indict the Jewish driver might simply, if wrongly, confirm one's conviction that Jews get special treatment and blacks, as Reverend Al Sharpton kept repeating, get "the short end of the stick."

Similarly, the Lubavitchers assessed the validity of black complaints from the perspective of their own distinctive notions of rationality. They parried black cries of Jewish influence with the query: So who's stopping you from organizing? Rabbi Butman insisted without apology, "An organized community is not synonymous with organized crime. That should be emulated, not destroyed. If blacks would like tips to organize, we'd be pleased to share. But you can't complain. You have an *obligation* to organize your community."

The statement could be read as a paternalistic impugning of black competence. It has the same edge as the Lubavitcher's definition of black grievances as self-evident jealousy; after all, as one leader observed, "The Jewish community does not have single-parent families." Such an unvarnished style of talking undoubtedly lacks a certain grace, and it surely fails to grasp the complex forces that impinge on the black poor and render the immigrant model of plucky striving of only partial and ambiguous relevance. Still, a lack of gentility is not the same thing as racism or blaming the victim. The statement at least had the virtue of not flinching from saying publicly what many Lubavitchers, and even liberals and black leaders, actually say privately: there is at least a tendency in black political culture to avoid collective responsibility. After all, why Lubavitchers wield the influence they do is not mysterious. They do what democratic theory says they should do: they energetically participate. Moreover, the black charge of powerlessness seems like an anachronistic ruse. The Crown Heights councilwoman was an Afro-Caribbean; the assemblyman from the area was a Caribbean; in 1991, the mayor and police commissioner were African Americans.

In some of its current versions, vernacular black nationalism has followed the line of cultivating resentment. But one Barbadian woman, although angry that the police did not charge the Jewish driver, asked, "Did the Jews make those black hoodlums take crack? What does looting sneakers and gold jewelry have to do with Gavin Cato's death?" This counterpoint has been a rising strain in black nationalist discourse: don't trash Korean grocery stores, let's start our own; picket crack houses rather than grocers "who don't look like us." On a black radio station, around the time of the Crown Heights explosion, Reverend Herbert Daughtry conceded that the problem was not the Jews but in the family. "What is it with us? We need to take a long hard look at *our* fragmentation, *our* own lethargy, *our* disillusionment with the system." The Lubavitchers were practicing ethnic power in a form that black power advocates would be happy to realize.

The Hasidim have used their power in the realm of real estate. Black militants seized on Jewish patrols among people of color and territorial expansion to support the imagery of a Jewish landgrab on the West Bank. In resonant language, they railed against this "conspiracy to steal our land (homes)." A Caribbean leader put it to me more simply: "The crux of the problem is economic, it's about housing: the Hasidim are desperate for space." The size of Lubavitcher families increases pressures to expand. The Caribbean influx has only added to the squeeze. But the real estate has remained constant. Over recent decades, the Jews have responded with zeal, aggressively getting city monies for renovating homes, sometimes making cash purchases at top-of-the-market prices and pressuring black homeowners to sell. The resentments created by such ferocious solicitation became so intense during Mayor Koch's tenure that he felt obliged to warn, "This type of persistent and unwelcome solicitation of homeowners . . . constitutes a form of harassment that can only lead to increased tension with the community."[6]

The Jews are convinced that, without them, Crown Heights might become another slum. We aren't the ones, they have argued, who mug and create the litter of crack vials. Besides, in a market economy, the best price gets the house. But the Jewish retort, with its tacit superiority and cool market logic, was not likely to assuage the resentment of less privileged blacks who could not afford the homes Jews were buying. Nor did it own up to the more ample resources the Jewish community can lay claim to. If the hardly Lockean Lubavitchers have viewed their own conduct as a way to advance communal interests, why were blacks wrong to see the Jewish advance as a detriment to *black* ethnic interests. Given the undeniable territorial squeeze, scarcity of good housing, and Lubavitcher acquisition of the best housing along President Street, the

Jewish advance toward the west and the east could easily take on the appearance of menacing encroachment.

For proud, dignified Caribbeans, many of whom embrace a virtually Anglophilic dislike of "rudeness," to knock on someone's door and ask to buy their home is disrespectful chutzpah. It seems to declare, "I want you to leave; I want the community for my own kind." As one man fumed, "They knocked on my door! And then they had the nerve to tell me, 'Why don't you sell? I have a need. My need is greater than yours.' I told him, 'I don't want to sell. This is my homestead.' And they still came back! They see nothing wrong with this aggressiveness."

The decrial of Jewish nerviness contained the elements of a broader symbolic struggle. The entire gestural style of the Lubavitchers is at odds with Caribbean manners. "They walk down the sidewalk seven-strong and push you into the gutter," complained one Trinidadian resident. "I have to stand my ground on my own sidewalk." This seeming pushiness on the streets is reinforced by the Lubavitchers' spatial assertion of their cultural presence. They rope off streets on the Sabbath and on High Holidays. A few weeks after the riots, a group of Lubavitchers started pounding on the hood of a West Indian doctor's car because he was driving past the synagogue on the Sabbath. In such a charged milieu, the black separatist cry "Whose streets, our streets" easily takes on broader resonance.

All of this can strike proud Caribbean immigrants and American blacks sensitive to slight as disrespect, even racist disrespect. Fear and dislike of blacks play some role in the rudeness of some Hasids. More importantly, many Lubavitchers display an apparent lack of tender sensitivity not only to blacks but to any non-Jews and even to Jews and their fellow Lubavitchers. Various factors account for this: ethnic aggressiveness untamed by assimilationist refinement, the presence of provincial recent immigrants, feelings of superiority created by a sense of chosenness, indifference to "goyim," the spiritual preoccupation of a messianic people whose mind is centered elsewhere, the pressures of hurrying to and from synagogue. But no single group in Crown Heights has a monopoly on rudeness. Young blacks sometimes greet Jewish pedestrians with icy stares; and blacks leaving the bars on Nostrand Street late at night often do not treat Jews trying to sleep with polite consideration.

The abrasions of daily life and ethnic jostling remind us of the delicacy of the balance between pluralism and difference. Rivalries of culture and class, power and real estate can easily upset it. In those moments, the outcome may depend not just on the fact of tension but on the moral and institutional mechanisms for regulating it. The buffer of trust and leaders with grace may determine whether mingling results in vendetta or accommodation. When such buffers are missing, misunderstandings grow and demagogues can distort. Back in 1991, Rabbi Schneerson's silence on the Cato death pained many Jews and outraged blacks. As *The Jewish Week* reported, Schneerson made cryptic remarks about the need to "care about non-Jews and the world at large," but his aides discouraged any effort to make racial harmony the missing link in a messianic vision. This was all pretty obscure stuff. What did get through to blacks via the tabloids were the callous comments of one rabbi, later disavowed by the central Hasidic command, that upheld the stereotype of stiff-necked Jews. He said Lubavitchers had nothing to apologize for. On the streets, this is called having an "attitude." If I were Gavin Cato's father, I might not respond with equanimity to such a statement, unless I knew of rival messages. And, indeed, there were rival messages; but the black activists, with their big and little lies, instead inflamed with rhetoric about "the arrogance of Jews." At the very first press conference after the riots, Rabbi Hecht lit two Yahrzeit (memorial) candles, one for Gavin Cato, and expressed his heartfelt condolences. Also, a delegation of Lubavitcher neighbors paid a condolence call on the Cato home and told Sherman Cato, Gavin's uncle, of their profound sorrow at the loss of a precious life.

In Brooklyn and the nation, the clashes of rising and falling groups will generate tribal heat. For the Caribbeans, class resentment, racial outrage, and anti-Semitism remain threats to the still-dominant versions of ethnic competition. Meanwhile, they will seek greater power. If that offends our sense of universalism, we need to remember that Lubavitchers have zealously tried to realize not what is good for humankind or for Jews as a whole, but for their special tribe of Jews. The Hasids' decision to march in the West Indian Day Parade right after the riots was not only an act of graciousness but a shrewd, if ambivalent, concession to the altered environment in which they must promote their interests.

The parade is the central public symbol of West Indian cultural affirmation, a carnival of steel-band music and riotous celebration. People work on their elaborate costumes for months. For years, it had galled Caribbeans that the Lubavitchers, who demand so much deference for their ceremonies, called for rerouting the parade so that it wouldn't pass the main yeshiva (seminary) on Eastern Parkway. Until right before the parade, some Lubavitchers, afraid of violence, were calling for postponing it. They must have been woefully ignorant of that old calypso tune, "Don't Change my Carnival."

In a healing move, Carlos Lezama, the head of the Parade Association, invited the Lubavitchers to participate. Momentarily, Brooklyn returned to its more benign form of tribalism. Pluralism here was not a love fest, but a pragmatic entente tinged with the submerged tensions of difference. The Lubavitchers were not really thrilled with the lasciviousness that is part of Carnival but violates orthodox taboos on immodesty. And still they worried about the Jew-haters out in the crowd. And Caribbean leaders quipped backstage, "Did you hear what happened to Rabbi Butman?" "No, I heard everything was quiet at Carnival," said another. "Yes, the Rabbi won the best costume award."

NOTES

1. This article is a revised version of a piece that originally appeared in *The New Republic*, 14 October 1991. For a more theoretical treatment of the Crown Heights incident, as well as the methodological problems involved in interpreting black anti-Semitism, see my "Reflections on Crown Heights: Interpretive Dilemmas and Black-Jewish Conflict," in *Anti-Semitism in America: Myths and Realities*, Jerome A. Chanes, ed. (New York: Birch Lane Press, 1995).

2. Reprinted in *The Jewish Press* 41, no. 36 (6–12 September 1991).

3. Peter Noel, "Crown Heights Burning," *The Village Voice*, 3 September 1991, p. 37.

4. Quoted in *New York Amsterdam News*, 14 September 1991, p. 1.

5. *Carib News*, 17 September 1991, p. 3.

6. Quoted in Jerome Mintz, *Hasidic People: A Place in the New World* (Cambridge, Mass.: Harvard University Press, 1991), p. 329.

5
_____

The Persistence of Anti-Asian Hatred

Gary Y. Okihiro

On the evening of October 24, 1871, a mob of about five hundred whites descended upon ''Nigger Alley,'' the location of Los Angeles' Chinatown, killed nineteen Chinese, seventeen of whom were lynched, looted over $30,000 in cash and personal property, and burned many of the shops and residences.[1] Two days later, the *Los Angeles Daily Star* described the scene of the devastation: ''The guard posted by the sheriff was kept on duty until daylight yesterday morning, at which hour those portions of the building to which the crowd had failed to penetrate were entered, and eight Chinamen and seven women found therein. Almost every compartment in the block has been ransacked; trunks, boxes, and locked receptacles of all kind broken open in a search for money and valuables. . . . It is stated that the pockets of the captured were robbed in many instances, whilst dangling from the improvised gallows.''

Over one hundred years later, at midday on April 30, 1992, a crowd and then a mob of mainly African Americans began burning and looting businesses and stores along Vermont Avenue, the site of Los Angeles' Koreatown. ''We fled for our safety,'' recalled Paul Yi, who spent the night at his parents' house in the suburbs. ''We heard the TV saying that blacks were gathering and coming northward.'' After the fires had cooled, one Korean American lay dead, forty-six were injured, and damage to about 2,000 Korean-American stores topped $400 million. Parts of Japantown were also hit, and Japanese-American businesses suffered more than $3 million in damages.

The Los Angeles riot of 1871 and the uprising of 1992 exemplify the persistence of anti-Asian hatred in America; and they were not the first, nor will they be the last instances of anti-Asianism within the American experience. Anti-Asianism's edge is sharp, because it cuts and delineates the line between "insider" and "outsider," those deemed members of the American community and those outside that privileged circle. Tagged as outsiders, Asians were the objects of race hatred: such was the unnamed Chinese American who, while running from the 1871 mob, was captured, dragged through the street, and hanged twice—the rope broke the first time—at New High Street in Los Angeles; the eight, terror-stricken Chinese, two of whom were mere boys, who were cornered by the mob that disregarded their pleas for mercy, kicked and beat them, and dragged them with ropes tied around their necks over the stone streets to their place of murder; and Chien Lee "Gene" Tong, a physician who had begged for his life in English and Spanish but was hanged and had one of his fingers cut off to get at the ring he wore.[2]

During the 1992 Los Angeles uprising, the sole Asian-American fatality, eighteen-year-old Edward Song Lee, died when he was mistakenly shot at the intersection of Third Street and Hobart Avenue by Korean-American gunmen perched on the rooftop intent on protecting their property because the police had failed to respond to their calls for help. H. Andrew Kim, board vice-chair of the Los Angeles Korean American Coalition, declared that Koreatown's burning taught Korean Americans "that the system we have trusted with a blind faith and the democratic institutions that we long revered even before we came to this shore are as vulnerable as the institutions that we have left behind." Ji-Yeon Yuhfill, a *New York Newsday* reporter, reflected upon the meanings of the 1992 uprising and noted the ambivalent position of Korean and Asian Americans. "America has never fully accepted us," she wrote, "and we, like the blacks, are marginalized socially, culturally, politically and economically. The resentment blacks feel at Korean merchants is echoed by the resentment whites and other groups feel at second-generation Asian Americans in the nation's best universities. While blacks burned down Korean stores on television, whites quietly set informal ceilings on the number of Asian American students in their schools."[3]

Anti-Asianism's persistence is not a mere academic problem. It is personal. When my wife and I were awakened in the early morning hours of Memorial Day, 1978, in Eureka, California, by the loud thud of a heavy boulder crashing through our front door, followed by the sound of screeching car tires, I was fully aware of the county's 1885 mass expulsion of Chinese Americans and the 1909 dynamiting of the Tsuchiya brothers' Eureka store. And when we and our two small children walked along the sidewalk in San Jose, California, on a hot summer's day in 1985 and three white men in a pickup truck drove by and yelled, "damned gooks!," I knew that in 1870 San Jose's Chinatown was burned completely, likely by arsonists, and that in 1942 all of the city's Japanese Americans were herded onto trains that took them to concentration camps. And when in 1991 a sales clerk at the Sears department store in Ithaca, New York, accused me of being "true to my nationality" when I, an American three generations deep, wondered aloud about the comparative quality of Japanese- and American-made products, I was painfully aware of the 1982 beating death in Detroit, Michigan, of Vincent Chin, a Chinese American, by two white autoworkers who had called him a "Jap" and had cursed him: "It's because of you motherfuckers that we're out of work."[4] Anti-Asianism's persistence is very personal.

Persistence, however, does not mean the same. The Los Angeles riot of 1871 was not the Los Angeles uprising of 1992. There were fundamental differences. In 1871, the lynching of Chinese Americans, the looting of their property, the burning of their stores followed the shooting death of a white man by a Chinese gunman, and the mob's intent was to inflict "frontier justice" upon the unruly, inferior race. Within the racial formation, codified in laws and practiced as custom, the mob—the majority—was simply exercising its privilege of power over those kept at a distance from that power—the minority. In 1992, the looting and destruction of Korean- and Japanese-American businesses followed the verdict of innocence for the white police officers indicted in the brutal beating of African-American motorist Rodney G. King. The uprising, for some, was an expression of powerlessness, of minority group membership, and not an exercise of power that was exemplified by the police officers, members of the majority, who wielded power with apparent impunity. But both the 1871 riot and the 1992 uprising illustrate, I think, the persistence and natures of anti-Asian hatred that position Asian Americans simultaneously as a minority, or as the "yellow peril," and as a minority set apart from other minorities, or as the "model minority."

The term "yellow peril" was probably coined in 1895 by German

Kaiser Wilhelm II, who framed the danger as a conflict between European civilization and Christianity and Asian barbarism and paganism. But the idea of the "yellow peril" long preceded the imperialist 1890s, its first seeds perhaps planted within the European imagination by the Mongol invasions of the thirteenth century and within America by the Chinese migration of the 1850s likened to a "peaceful invasion." I am intrigued that the rise of "yellow peril" rhetoric was preceded and accompanied by European and European-American expansion and colonization into the Third World and by the reciprocal movement of peoples and products from the peripheries into the core, resulting in what author Salman Rushdie has aptly called the "empire within."[5] Having just invaded and absorbed Mexican territory and incorporated its native peoples through the 1848 Treaty of Guadalupe Hidalgo, Americans sought to preserve California for its "native sons," exclusive of African Americans, Asian migrants, and even the indigenous Indians, Mexicans, and Californios or Spanish Mexicans.

California's 1850 foreign miners' tax originally aimed at Latin-American immigrants was, by 1852, directed principally at the Chinese. On May 8, 1852, in the Columbia mining district of Tuolumne County, American miners condemned the "capitalists, ship-owners and merchants and others" who profited from "this Asiatic inundation that threatens to roll over the State," and resolved to "take the matter into their [the miners] own hands" by prohibiting Asians and Pacific Islanders from mining in the district.[6] And in 1854, the state's supreme court ruled that, like Indians and Africans, Chinese could not testify in court for or against whites, to protect the state, according to the ruling, from the "actual and present danger" of "a race of people whom nature has marked as inferior, and who are incapable of progress or intellectual development beyond a certain point . . . differing in language, opinions, color, and physical conformation; between whom and ourselves nature has placed an impassable difference."[7]

Los Angeles, home to Yang-na Indians, was colonized as a Spanish outpost by a contingent of forty-four settlers and four soldiers in about 1781. Among the settlers, "whose blood was a mixture of Indian and Negro with traces of a few Spanish" according to historian Hubert Howe Bancroft, was a Chinese named Antonio Rodriguez, who had probably converted to Catholicism in Manila, migrated to Mexico, and headed one of the original families that established Spain's Los Angeles pueblo.[8] By 1870, the city of Los Angeles numbered 5,728, 172 of whom were Chinese. Employed as servants to whites, the Chinese also operated merchandise stores and laundries that were patronized by whites. Thus, although comprising a mere 3 percent of the city's population, nearly half of whom lived along the one-block roadway named Negro Alley, the Chinese were not insulated from the whites of Los Angeles, and, in the case of servants and cooks, they had close and intimate relationships with whites.

The position of Chinese merchants revealed class distinctions among the Chinese of Los Angeles and showed an aspect of the relations between white and yellow. White patrons purchased goods from Chinese merchants and used their stores as casual meeting places to talk and swap stories. Chinese stores constituted sites of cultural contact, contestation, and exchange. Whites thereby designated the business class as the spokesmen for the Chinese, most of whom were of the working class, and the merchants became conduits of information from white society to the Chinese.[9] Yo Hing, for example, changed his name to Joseph Hinton and was described by a white contemporary as "a well-to-do merchant of wide repute and of great authority among his countrymen, being an agent of one of the great Chinese companies in this city."[10]

Having access to capital, the merchants employed retail clerks for their shops, but also doormen, dealers, bagmen, cooks, janitors, madames, and henchmen for their gambling houses and places of prostitution that lined Negro Alley and made it notorious. Some of the proceeds from those activities were skimmed off by whites, including police officers, who formed profitable partnerships with Chinese merchants. Yo Hing (or Joseph Hinton), head of the Hong Chow Association and proprietor of a cigar manufacturing firm, and Sam Yuen, head of the Nin Yung Association and owner of a retail business, were rivals for influence among both Chinese and whites; they pursued their objects through legal means, but also through bribery, extortion, kidnapping, and murder.

Four days before the riot, in an American-style wedding before a judge, a member of the Hong Chow Association, possibly Yo Hing, married Ya Hit, a prostitute who allegedly had been abducted by the Hong Chows and claimed by the Nin Yung Association. By using the American institution of marriage, Yo Hing acquired "property" and labor valued at $2,500, Ya Hit's supposed price, while frustrating the usual strategy for redress open to Sam Yuen. Commonly, the "aggrieved" obtained a warrant for the arrest of the woman who was considered his property, offered a reward for her return, awaited her capture, and reclaimed her by paying her bail. The American judicial system, thus employed, was an active and willing accomplice in the subordination and exploitation of Chinese women and the empowerment and accumulation of Chinese men of the propertied class. Referring to a Chinese prostitute, the police openly acknowledged that "the woman arrested . . . has been several times arrested in a similar manner, and her possession as often changed hands from one Company to that of another—through the instrumentality of law."[11]

Because of the money involved, whites apparently scrambled to get a piece of the action. Less than a year before the 1871 riot, Los Angeles city marshal William C. Warren and one of his officers, Joseph Dye, quarreled and fought over a reward offered by a Chinese company for the capture of a prostitute wanted on a bogus warrant. In full view of dozens of witnesses, Dye drew his revolver and shot Warren in the groin, leaped upon the fallen marshal, and bit him with his teeth while beating him with his pistol. Warren later died of his wounds. And two police officers, or one-third of the city's entire police force, were "the avowed friends" of Sam Yuen, head of the Nin Yung Company, and received, a few days before the riot, "a beautiful gift, consisting of Chinese embroidery" from Yuen "as a testimonial of their appreciation of services rendered," according to the *Los Angeles Star.*[12]

Tension built between the Hong Chows and Nin Yungs in the days following the marriage of Ya Hit. Both sides collected arms, and Sam Yuen apparently offered a $1,000 reward for Yo Hing's head. On Monday morning, October 23, two shots were fired at Yo Hing, both missing their target, as he walked along Negro Alley.[13] The factions prepared for open war, and throughout the day threats were shouted across the alley and few people ventured out onto the street. Responding to the sound of gunfire on the afternoon of the 24th, a police officer rushed to Negro Alley and found a Nin Yung man with a mortal neck wound. Sam Yuen and another Nin Yung gunman emerged from a building and called to the officer presumably for help, but the officer instead charged toward Yuen with a pistol in hand, calling for a white citizen in the area to help him capture the Chinese. Yuen and his companion, thinking that the officer had been bribed by the Hong Chows, fired wildly as they ran for cover inside. Their bullets missed their marks but struck and wounded superficially two who stood in a gathering crowd of whites and possibly Mexicans. The officer followed Yuen into the building, was greeted with bullets, retreated to the porch with a shoulder wound, and blew his whistle for help.[14]

Another officer arrived at the scene with Robert Thompson, a rancher, and the pair commenced firing into the building. While emptying his pistol, Thompson approached the front door and was met by a hail of bullets fired from inside. As he staggered backward with a bullet in his chest, Thompson muttered "I am killed" and died about an hour later in a drugstore two blocks away on Main Street. The police chief arrived about the time that Thompson was shot, and he ordered the entire building surrounded by men from the crowd and directed them to shoot any Chinese trying to escape. He then left the area. Similarly, the sheriff, mayor, and several other police officers visited the scene, saw the rapidly growing crowd, and left or stood idly by.

News of Thompson's death at about six o'clock spread throughout the city and rumors that the Negro Alley Chinese were "killing whites wholesale" fed the flames of hatred. Some in the crowd tried unsuccessfully to flush out the Chinese by directing a fire hose at the building. In the commotion, Tuck Wong, who had been hiding in a building across the alley, made a dash to escape but was captured; as he struggled to free himself, someone tried to plunge a broken sword into him shouting, "Oh you Chinaman, you had a gun!" Two policemen intervened and took Wong into custody, but as they led him away toward the station, the surging crowd overpowered them and seized Wong. The owners of a bookstore furnished the crowd with some rope, and Wong was soon hanging from a corral gate just across from the St. Athanasius Episcopal Church. A few amused themselves by swinging his body and smashing his head against the upright posts.

As the police stood in the background, the crowd riddled the buildings of Negro Alley with bullets. When two Chinese women emerged from one of the houses, the crowd, including an officer, fired at them, wounding one and driving them back into the building. At about nine o'clock, long after darkness had settled on the city and the gas lamps had been lit along Negro Alley, several men climbed onto the roof of the surrounded building, chopped holes into the flat roof using axes, and fired through them. Two Chinese ran out and were quickly cut down by gunfire. The mob then stormed the building, searched and ransacked the apartments therein, and found dozens of Chinese men, women, and children.

The bodies of some who were already dead were thrown out onto the street where they were kicked and mutilated and dragged off to be hanged. Others found alive were besieged and hanged with clothesline provided by a woman who ran a boarding house across the street from John Goller's wagon shop, a favored place of hanging for the lynch mob. Goller's protest against the mob's use of his porch roof went unheeded.

One of the men who helped haul up the bodies danced a jig on the roof and reportedly sang a "yellow peril" tune: "Come on, boys, patronize home trade!" he intoned. Meanwhile, the diffident police notwithstanding, looters worked through the remains of the Chinese homes, running off with bolts of silk, sacks of rice, bottles of wine, and other valuables.

Not all whites participated in the carnage. Some, like officers Emil Harris and George Gard, defended Sam Yuen's store against looters because they profited from Yuen's patronage. But others acted altruistically and courageously: Robert M. Widney, a schoolteacher, real estate agent, and later a judge, risked his life to wrest four Chinese from the clutches of the mob; and Henry Hazard and J. M. Baldwin tried to reason with the crowd despite insults and threats of violence. And still others, like Judge W. H. Gray, hid Chinese in their homes from the mob. By eleven o'clock, the riot had run its course.

In the riot's aftermath, hoodlums and thugs, the Irish and Mexicans, and ineffectual police were blamed by the press, popular opinion, and a grand jury as the culprits in the massacre that, in the words of the grand jury's report, "disgraced our city, and has cast reproach upon the people of Los Angeles County." Ultimately, no Chinese was imprisoned for the events of October 24, and eight whites were found guilty of manslaughter and given sentences of two to six years, leading the *Los Angeles Daily News* to exult: "It had been the universal belief of the entire country that a conviction of the perpetrators of the outrage that cast a blot upon the fair name of our city could never be obtained in this county!" Still, after having served just one year in prison, all of the convicted killers were released on a technicality—that the original indictment had failed to establish that the victim, Chien Lee "Gene" Tong, had been murdered in the first place.[15]

The Los Angeles riot of 1871, it seems to me, clearly showed Asians to be members of a minority group, despite the sympathy and friendship of certain whites, and despite the relative privileges of the merchant class who employed the legal system for their own ends and who were shielded from unmitigated political and police harassment. Regardless, they were all subject to mob violence in the streets, because they were, as a racial group, excluded from full membership in the American community. Thus, Sam Yuen's stash of $6,000, hidden in his store and guarded over by officers Harris and Gard, disappeared the night of the riot; and Yuen's suit against the city for the losses he had incurred because of, he claimed, police ineptitude was dismissed by a jury that held that Yuen had instigated and participated in the riot.[16] Also, despite one's class position, all Chinese were barred from testifying against whites and were thereby easy, unthreatening targets of white violence. The police officers, according to their testimony, "felt during the night of the riot that it would have been legally useless to have made any arrests because the victims of the mob were Chinese and therefore, clearly outside the protection of statutory law."[17] The Chinese, despite the class and gender privileges enjoyed by some of them, were the objects of race hatred, as minorities.

The Los Angeles uprising of 1992 positioned Asians as a minority apart from other minorities, or as the "model minority." Sociologist William Petersen probably coined the term "model minority" in a timely essay entitled, "Success Story, Japanese American Style," published in the *New York Times Magazine* on January 6, 1966 (p. 21), in the aftermath of the 1965 Watts riot. "Asked which of the country's ethnic minorities has been subjected to the most discrimination and the worst injustices," he wrote, "very few persons would even think of answering: 'The Japanese Americans.' Yet, if the question refers to persons alive today, that may well be the correct reply. Like the Negroes," he argued, "the Japanese have been the object of color prejudice. Like the Jews, they have been seen as the agents of an overseas enemy. Conservatives, liberals and radicals, local sheriffs, the Federal Government and the Supreme Court have cooperated in denying them their elementary rights— most notoriously in their World War II evacuation to internment camps."

Petersen elevated Japanese Americans as "models" for other minorities, who had, through "cumulative degradation," become "problem minorities." Even after the formal end of segregation and discrimination, he contended, minorities maintained an attitude of "either self-defeating apathy or a hatred so all-consuming as to be self-destructive. For all the well-meaning programs and countless scholarly studies now focused on the Negro, we barely know how to repair the damage that the slave traders started." But the history of Japanese Americans, countered Petersen, defies that generalization about America's minorities. "Every attempt to hamper their progress resulted only in enhancing their determination to succeed. Even in a country whose patron saint is the Horatio Alger hero, there is no parallel to this success story." Moreover, Petersen claimed, "by any criterion of good citizenship that we choose, the Japanese Americans are better than any other group in our society including native-born whites."

Some five years after Petersen's pronouncement, *Newsweek* declared that Japanese Americans had "outwhited the whites," and other Asian-

American ethnic groups joined the ranks of the "model minority." In an article published in the same year as Petersen's essay, *U.S. News & World Report* praised Chinese-American success: "Visit Chinatown U.S.A.," the report contended, "and you find an important racial minority pulling itself up from hardship and discrimination to become a model of self-respect and achievement in today's America."[18] And more recent articles in *Newsweek, Time,* the *New Republic,* the *New York Times Magazine,* and *Fortune* name Korean, Asian Indian, and Southeast Asian Americans as exemplars of a generalized Asian American success story.[19]

The idea of the "model minority" posits a compatibility, if not identity, between key elements of Asian and Anglo-American culture, and, thus, instead of representing an "alien culture" as described by Petersen in the 1960s, Anglicized Asian culture reaffirms WASPish attributes of the work ethic, education, family values, and self-help in the 1980s and 1990s. According to neoconservatives, Asian Americans exemplify the need to return to the basic principles that have made this nation great. In articles titled "Confucian Work Ethic," "A Drive to Excel," "A Formula for Success," "Why Asians Are Going to the Head of the Class," and "America's Super Minority," commentators echo economist Thomas Sowell's contention: "Asian parents are teaching a lesson that otherwise isn't being taught in America anymore. When you see a study that says Asian kids study harder than white and black kids and are getting better grades, it tells you something."[20]

Having gotten the message, some African Americans believe that "model" Asians benefit from special privileges denied to them and are complicit with whites in the subjugation and exploitation of blacks. "It is not accidental that Koreans control the Fruit and Vegetable market," alleged a 1990 flyer of the December 12th Movement in urging an African boycott of Korean stores in Brooklyn. "The Korean merchants are agents of the U.S. government in their conspiracy to destabilize the economy of our community. They are rewarded by the government and financed by big business." The St. Louis African Merchants Association posted flyers urging Africans to "boycott Asian merchants who sell imitation black and Afrocentric products." African communities, the association claimed, were threatened by "Asian profiteers," who "steal our cultural creativity and stunt the growth of black business."

"It is . . . no surprise that the Korean-owned liquor stores, furniture warehouses and beauty-supply shops are hit," reported Ruben Martinez of scenes from the 1992 Los Angeles uprising. "Black-Korean tension

Thousands of anti-abortion demonstrators marched in Washington, D.C. on the seventh anniversary of the Supreme Court decision recognizing women's constitutional right to abortion. Courtesy of UPI/Corbis-Bettmann.

Students and religious leaders gather on the steps of the Mississippi Capitol in Jackson, Tuesday, November 30, 1993 to protest not being allowed to use school facilities for prayer. Photo by Tannen Maury. Courtesy of AP/Wide World Photos.

Private Korean security guards ready for patrol duty in Los Angeles' Koreatown district during the Rodney King Trial. Korean businesses were targeted during the riots that followed the 1992 trial. Courtesy of Reuters/Lee Celano/Archive Photos.

A coalition of over 40 community and human rights groups organized a demonstration in San Francisco in December 1994 against Proposition 187, anti-immigration legislation in California aimed at controlling the flood of illegal immigrants into the state. Photo by Darryl Bush. Courtesy of AP/Wide World Photos.

Paul Hill, former minister and abortion opponent, waits on death row at Florida State Prison in December 1994 for murdering an abortion doctor and an unarmed women's clinic escort in an attempt to thwart legal abortions at a clinic in Pensacola, Florida in July 1994. Photo by Mark Foley. Courtesy of AP/Wide World Photos.

Senator Diane Feinstein barely survived re-election to the U.S. Senate after declaring her opposition to California's Proposition 187, the so-called illegal aliens bill, which overwhelmingly won passage in the fall of 1994. Here she is announcing her opposition to the bill despite admitting that it could cost her the race. Courtesy of Reuters/Blake Sell/Archive Photos.

was ready to explode. 'I've been waiting nine years for this day!' exults an African-American man . . . as the fishmarket across the street is looted. 'I owned that place until I had to sell out to the Koreans.' " "The black man can't get a $100,000 loan but the Korean can come into the neighborhood and buy us out, sky-high sales," a looter told *Village Voice* reporter Peter Noel. "I'm glad we burned that [referring to a Korean-owned store] down." Urban League leader John Mack, appearing on ABC's "Nightline," asserted that Koreans "are in America now" and had to learn and conform to its ways, and African-American columnist Julianne Malveaux charged that some Asians enjoyed their status as "honorary whites" and adopted racist ideology: "I understand that when people come to this racist society, they emulate its values," wrote Malveaux. "I've seen people here who can barely speak English, yet they can say 'nigger.' "[21]

Perhaps the clinching evidence of Asian and white collusion for some African-American rioters was the probationary sentence meted out by white judge Joyce A. Karlin to Soon Ja Du, a Korean grocer whose videotaped shooting of Latasha Harlins was repeatedly juxtaposed (along with images of gun-wielding Korean merchants) by the media with the videotaped beating of Rodney King. Writing of Los Angeles's African Americans, reporter Peter Noel surmised: "Most agree that the King verdict, coming on top of the suspended sentence given to a Korean store owner last year for the shooting death of 15-year-old Latasha Harlins, a black girl, was too much to bear." And two men told reporter Jim Crogan: "It wasn't just the Rodney King verdict. It's the whole thing, the shooting of Latasha Harlins and the lack of jail time for that Korean woman. The Koreans treat us bad. You go into their stores and they treat you like, 'Give me your money and get the fuck out of here.' That's not right. They treat us like dogs."[22]

Despite those alleged privileges of Asians, specifically Koreans, five Korean stores in Los Angeles were firebombed during a six-month period in 1991, and Yong Tae Park died on December 15, 1991, of bullet wounds received during a robbery. He was the seventh Korean store owner killed by African suspects that year. During 1993, forty-six Koreans were shot, nineteen fatally, and all of the assailants were either African Americans or Latinos.[23] "We live with the threat of being robbed and killed every day that we open up our stores," declared Annie Cho, executive director of the Korean-American Grocers Association. "It's an occupational hazard."[24] In truth, Soon Ja Du, charged with voluntary manslaughter in the death of Latasha Harlins, had been threatened repeatedly over an eighteen-month period before the fatal shooting by alleged gang members, two of whom were sentenced to prison terms for threats and thefts in Du's store; and during the altercation, seconds before Du picked up her pistol, the taller and heavier Harlins punched and knocked the store owner down several times.[25]

Koreans took up arms to protect their property during the civil unrest "because of the failure of local and state law-enforcement forces to respond to requests for help," according to *Korea Times* reporter Yong Wha Kim. "Why did the LA police not respond to the repeated request of Korean-Americans for assistance in protecting their businesses, when at the same time they were so quick to guard other sections of the city like Hollywood?" Kim asked.[26] As of July 1993, fifteen months later, 45 percent of Korean businesses destroyed in the uprising remained closed, and 21 percent of Korean victims risked homelessness because of having lost their entire means of livelihood. Significant numbers, according to the study, still suffered mental and health problems from causes related to the civil disturbance.[27] "Some of us thought we were participating in the political process in a way that was meaningful," reflected attorney Angela Oh. "But when it came down to our hour of need, it became very clear that our participation and contributions were perhaps not very meaningful."[28]

Still, Asians have benefited from their location as middling minorities between black and white. Asian Americans, the majority of whom have immigrated since 1965, have had doors open to them because of the African- (and Asian-) American civil rights struggle. Asian Americans haven't been totally attentive to or appreciative of that debt, and recognition of a common history and condition by Asians and Africans alike has been painfully slow and regrettably fuzzy. Further, as sociologists Ivan Light and Edna Bonacich have shown, Asian entrepreneurs are both victims and perpetrators, exploited and exploiters, mediating between capital and labor.[29] Asian Americans must be honest with themselves about their relative privileges and complicities, about some who profit from their assigned status as America's "model minority" and who gain comfort in their hierarchies and racialisms. At the same time, consigned to the middle ground, Asians occupy a precarious perch within the U.S. racial formation.[30]

The idea of the "yellow peril" positions Asians as a minority group, exemplified by the Los Angeles riot of 1871. Exclusion laws that bolted the door to Asian immigration, antimiscegenation laws that secured the racial boundaries, and economic, social, and educational segregation sought to mitigate the imagined peril to the state by excluding Asians from community membership. As stated in the Naturalization Act of 1790, citizenship through naturalization would be limited to "free white persons" or the "worthy part of mankind," and the act, as interpreted by U.S. Supreme Court associate justice George Sutherland in the court's 1922 ruling on the application of Japanese-American Takao Ozawa for U.S. citizenship, reserved membership to whites only and not to "the appellant [who] is clearly of a race which is not Caucasian, and therefore belongs entirely outside the zone on the negative side."[31]

The idea of the "model minority," in contrast, situates Asians as a minority apart from other minorities, as revealed in the 1992 Los Angeles uprising. They are "just like" or even "better than" whites. Anglicized Asian-American culture enables easy assimilation and prosperity, unlike other minority cultures of poverty and victimization; and Asian-American responses to past discrimination have been positive, whereby hardship only heightened their determination to succeed, unlike the negative, "self-defeating apathy" and "hatred" of "problem minorities," according to some commentators. A *Wall Street Journal* and NBC News poll conducted in the spring of 1991 showed that a majority of Americans believed that there was no discrimination against Asian Americans, and some held that Asian Americans received "too many special advantages." Among those supposed "special advantages," no doubt, is the cultural edge that Asians presumably possess which enables them to succeed in America and dominate the world economy, as purported by a number of contemporary authors.

But the twentieth-century notion of Asian-American success, like the nineteenth-century exclusion of Asians from equal protection under the law, rendered Asians easy, obvious targets of white (and black and brown) violence. Asians can work too hard, study overmuch, stick together, and, as "racial tribes," "flood" our markets and displace workers, "flood" our schools and displace students, and "flood" our land with ghettoes of Chinatowns, Koreatowns, and Little Saigons. "Model" Asians exhibit the same singleness of purpose, patience and endurance, cunning, fanaticism, and ethnic loyalty seen in Mongol soldiers—embodiments of the "yellow peril"—by Marco Polo. ("They are capable of supporting every kind of privation. . . . No people on earth can surpass them in fortitude under difficulties, nor show greater patience under wants of every kind. They are perfectly obedient to their chiefs, and are maintained at small expense," Polo had written in 1275.)[32] Asian workers and students, maintained at little expense and almost robot-like, labor and study for hours on end without human needs for relaxation, fun, and pleasure; and M.I.T. becomes "Made in Taiwan" and U.C.L.A., "University of Caucasians Living among Asians."[33] A visitor to southern California chose his words carefully: "Asians in greater L.A. were known," he wrote, "with a mixture of admiration and fear, as drones, fierce in their commercial ambitions and still fiercer in their insistence that their children excel in school."[34]

Anti-Asian hatred in our time arises from a context of domestic fractures and international contests involving the decline of the Atlantic and rise of the Pacific economy, the massive and rapid immigration of Latinos and Asians, a growing diversity of America's people, and multiculturalism in the schools. By the year 2050, the U.S. Census Bureau predicts that whites will decrease to 53 percent of the American population, down from 75 percent in 1992. Latinos will comprise 21 percent; Africans, 15 percent; Asians, 10 percent; and American Indians, 1 percent. "I pick up the telephone and call the local garage," said West Virginia senator Robert C. Byrd. "I can't understand the person on the other side of the line. I'm not sure he can understand me. They're all over the place, and they don't speak English. Do we want more of this?"[35] And despite denials to the contrary, "they" and those who "don't speak English" are code words for racial minorities—Latinos, Asians, and Africans—who have been immigrating at rates several times over that of Europeans. As Peter Brimelow, a senior editor at *Forbes* magazine, observed, the immigration service waiting room was like the subway, "an underworld that is almost entirely colored."[36] For the majority, the global realignments and the empire within threaten America's economic and political borders and its cultural core.

Integral to that relation between majority and minority have been the relations among minority groups. The parameters established by the dominant class, together with migration, demographic shifts, and racial politics, have led to conflicts among America's peoples of color. African boycotts of Asian stores employed black nationalism as a means to advance the economic and political interests of certain classes of blacks by politicizing and unifying the divergent class and ethnic divisions among African Americans in the face of a common "other."[37] Likewise, directing hatred against Koreans in the 1992 Los Angeles uprising failed to dispel the hegemonies that repressed African aspirations. "Black young people need to understand that it is not the Korean-American small merchant who denies capital for investment in the black community, controls the banks and financial institutions or commits police brutality against blacks and Latinos,'' wrote political scientist Manning Marable. ''There may be legitimate complaints between the two groups. But such misdirected anger makes a unified response to race and class oppression virtually impossible.''[38] Whether emanating from the dominant class or from subordinate groups, anti-Asianism is alive and well.

The question of persistence, I believe, has something to do with the functional value of those assignations, those positionalities—''yellow peril'' and ''model minority''—that appear polar but, in reality, form a single continuum. I do not agree that anti-Asian hatred is simply an irrational or instinctual reaction; I do not hold that anti-Asian hatred is simply situational or circumstantial; I do not believe that anti-Asian hatred is simply confined to quirky individuals or fringe hate groups. Anti-Asianism's persistence, I think, argues for its utility to those who create, perpetuate, and deploy it. Similarly, racism's persistence testifies to its functional value in the social equation. Its forms, however, the forms of anti-Asianism and racism, change to suit the purposes of the moving social relations.

But a study of anti-Asianism's persistence, its natures and functions, gives cause for hope, even optimism. Because if anti-Asianism—if racism—is a purposeful construction, it is just as susceptible to a purposeful deconstruction. If we can build social institutions and relations with the brick and mortar of privilege and repression, we can also rebuild them without those tools and materials. If we can learn racism and prejudice, we can also unlearn racism and prejudice. And therein rests our responsibility—as scholars, as students, as members of the human community. Anti-Asianism's persistence is not a mere academic problem. It is very personal.

NOTES

1. William R. Locklear, ''The Celestials and the Angels: A Study of the Anti-Chinese Movement in Los Angeles to 1882,'' *Historical Society of Southern California Quarterly* 42, no. 3 (September 1960): 244. Locklear argues, nonetheless, that the mob action was not an indication of an anti-Chinese movement in Los Angeles.

2. C. P. Dorland, ''Chinese Massacre at Los Angeles in 1871,'' *Annual Publication of the Historical Society of Southern California* (1894), pp. 23–24.

3. *Korea Times*, June 29, 1992, p. 6.

4. Ronald Takaki, *Strangers from a Different Shore: A History of Asian Americans* (Boston: Little, Brown and Company, 1989), p. 481.

5. Salman Rushdie, "The New Empire within Britain," *New Society*, December 9, 1982.

6. Alexander McLeod, *Pigtails and Gold Dust* (Caldwell, Idaho: Caxton Publishers, 1947), p. 67.

7. Quoted in Cheng-Tsu Wu, ed., *"Chink!" A Documentary History of Anti-Chinese Prejudice in America* (New York: Meridian, 1972), p. 42.

8. Richard Griswold del Castillo, *The Los Angeles Barrio, 1850–1890: A Social History* (Berkeley: University of California Press, 1979), pp. 4–5; and Raymond Lou, "The Chinese American Community of Los Angeles, 1870–1900: A Case of Resistance, Organization and Participation," Ph.D. diss., University of California, Irvine, 1982, pp. 20–21.

9. Lou, "Chinese American Community," pp. 28–29.

10. Dorland, "Chinese Massacre," p. 22; and Lou, "Chinese American Community," p. 28.

11. Paul M. De Falla, "Lantern in the Western Sky," Part 1, *Historical Society of Southern California Quarterly* 42, no. 1 (March 1960): p. 67; and Dorland, "Chinese Massacre," p. 22.

12. Paul M. De Falla, "Lantern in the Western Sky," Part 2, *Historical Society of Southern California Quarterly* 42, no. 2 (June 1960): 168–69.

13. Dorland, "Chinese Massacre," p. 23.

14. This account of the riot is taken from De Falla, "Lantern in the Western Sky," Part 1, pp. 72–88; and ibid., Part 2, pp. 162–64, 169–70. See also, Dorland, "Chinese Massacre," pp. 22–26; Marco R. Newmark, "Calle de los Negros and the Chinese Massacre of 1871," *Historical Society of Southern California Quarterly* 26, nos. 2 and 3 (June–September 1944): 97–98; Locklear, "Celestials and the Angels," pp. 239–56; and Maurice H. Newmark and Marco R. Newmark, eds., *Sixty Years in Southern California, 1853–1913* (New York: Knickerbocker Press, 1916), pp. 432–35.

15. De Falla, "Lantern in the Western Sky," Part 2, pp. 174, 179, 184.

16. Ibid., pp. 168, 182–83.

17. Ibid., p. 170.

18. *U.S. News & World Report*, December 26, 1966, p. 73.

19. For an analysis of some of these articles, see Keith Osajima, "Asian Americans as the Model Minority: An Analysis of the Popular Press Image in the 1960's and 1980's," in *Reflections on Shattered Windows: Promises and Prospects for Asian American Studies*, Gary Y. Okihiro et al., eds. (Pullman: Washington State University Press, 1988), pp. 165–74.

20. *New York Times Magazine*, August 3, 1986.

21. *Inside the L.A. Riots* (Institute for Alternative Journalism), pp. 32–33, 49, 94.

22. Ibid., pp. 37, 48.

23. *Korea Times*, May 4, 1994, p. 1.

24. *Inside the L.A. Riots*, p. 95.

25. *Korea Times*, September 15, 1991, pp. 1, 6; and October 21, 1991, pp. 1, 7.

26. *Inside the L.A. Riots*, p. 95.

27. *Korea Times*, July 28, 1993, p. 1. See also Elaine H. Kim, "Home Is Where the Han Is: A Korean American Perspective on the Los Angeles Upheavals," in *Reading Rodney King, Reading Urban Uprising*, Robert Gooding-Williams, ed. (New York: Routledge, 1993), pp. 215–35.

28. Quoted in Seth Mydans, "Koreans Rethink Life in Los Angeles," *New York Times*, June 21, 1992, p. 16. For an account of coalition-building between Korean and African Americans in Los Angeles, see Elaine H. Kim, "Between Black and White: An Interview with Bong Hwan Kim," in *The State of Asian America: Activism and Resistance in the 1990s*, Karin Aguilar-San Juan, ed. (Boston: South End Press, 1994), pp. 71–100.

29. Ivan Light and Edna Bonacich, *Immigrant Entrepreneurs: Koreans in Los Angeles, 1965–1982* (Berkeley: University of California Press, 1988).

30. On the racial and political meanings of the 1992 Los Angeles uprising, see Michael Omi and Howard Winant, "The Los Angeles 'Race Riot' and Contemporary U.S. Politics," and Sumi K. Cho, "Korean Americans vs. African Americans: Conflict and Construction," in *Reading Rodney King*, Gooding-Williams, ed., pp. 97–114, 196–211.

31. Frank F. Chuman, *The Bamboo People: The Law and Japanese-Americans* (Del Mar, Calif.: Publisher's Inc., 1976), pp. 70–71.

32. *The Travels of Marco Polo the Venetian* (London: J. M. Dent, 1908), p. 128.

33. For a critique of the "model minority" stereotype, see Takaki, *Strangers from a Different Shore*, pp. 474–84; and Sucheng Chan, *Asian Americans: An Interpretive History* (Boston: Twayne, 1991), p. 151.

34. David Rieff, *Los Angeles: Capital of the Third World* (New York: Simon & Schuster, 1991), p. 151.

35. Quoted in Deborah Sontag, "Calls to Restrict Immigration Come from Many Quarters," *New York Times*, December 13, 1992, p. 5E.

36. Ibid. See also Peter Brimelow, *Alien Nation: Common Sense about America's Immigration Disaster* (New York: Random House, 1995).

37. Heon Cheol Lee, "The Dynamics of Black-Korean Conflict: A Korean American Perspective," paper presented at the 1994 Annual Meeting of the Association for Asian American Studies, University of Michigan, April 7, 1994.

38. *Inside the L.A. Riots*, p. 83.

BIBLIOGRAPHY

Aguilar-San Juan, Karin, ed. *The State of Asian America: Activism and Resistance in the 1990s*. Boston: South End Press, 1994.

Asian Women United of California, ed. *Making Waves: An Anthology of Writings by and about Asian American Women.* Boston: Beacon Press, 1989.

Chan, Sucheng. *Asian Americans: An Interpretive History.* Boston: Twayne, 1991.

Espiritu, Yen Le. *Asian American Women and Men: Labor, Laws, and Love.* Thousand Oaks, Calif.: Sage, 1996.

Gooding-Williams, Robert, ed. *Reading Rodney King, Reading Urban Uprising.* New York: Routledge, 1993.

Kim, Elaine H. *Asian American Literature: An Introduction to the Writings and Their Social Context.* Philadelphia: Temple University Press, 1982.

Okihiro, Gary Y. *Margins and Mainstreams: Asians in American History and Culture.* Seattle: University of Washington Press, 1994.

Takaki, Ronald. *Strangers from a Different Shore: A History of Asian Americans.* Boston: Little, Brown and Company, 1989.

Wong, Sau-ling Cynthia. *Reading Asian American Literature: From Necessity to Extravagance.* Princeton, N.J.: Princeton University Press, 1993.

6

The Dynamics of American Intergroup Conflict and Responses to Bigotry

Philip Perlmutter

All too often intergroup conflicts in America are discussed as if they were an exception to human group behavior, or as if America were structurally bigoted, or as if all victims reacted equally to prejudice and discrimination. Neither history nor psychology is that simple.

The history of American intergroup relations and conflict is filled with contradictions between idealism and greed, cruelty and kindness, and despair and hope, wherein there was ever increasing respect for intergroup differences and elimination of inequities in equal treatment of minorities. It is also a history of continuing immigration and diversity of people, whether of Siberians thousands of years ago crossing the Bering Strait and moving to the tip of South America, or of small boatloads of English dissenters, indentured servants, and jailbirds coming to New England and Virginia, or of today's legal and illegal immigrants jetting here from all corners of the earth.

Third, it is a history of interethnic, interracial, and interfaith competition and conflict, with heavy dosages of cultural, racial, and military triumphalism, among the early white European invaders (English, French, Spanish, Dutch, and Swedish); between them and Indians; among Indian tribes; between whites and blacks; and between all whites—whether immigrant or native-born—and Mexicans, Alaskans,

Pacific and Caribbean Islanders, and Asians. To one degree or another, each minority group was exposed to some form of emotional, behavioral, and institutional prejudice, and each group reacted differently.

If being murdered and robbed of home are the worst that can befall a group, then Indians were the biggest victims, followed by blacks, who were the only group brought to America against their will as slaves, separated in Africa or America from their families, and not allowed to perpetuate their customs and languages. Mexicans throughout the Southwest were made strangers in their own land, as were native Hawaiians, both of whose lands were taken by trickery and conquest. Alaskan natives were not asked whether they wanted their land sold by Russia to America. Asians were viewed as perils by native-born and immigrants alike, with the Chinese the only group specifically excluded by law from coming here.

Contrary to popular or radical writing, white Europeans did not introduce intergroup conflict to America. It existed among the aborigines long before they came, which partially explains the movement south of Asians and Indians, who not only sought food, but fled from other groups or pursued plunder from those in front of them.

Columbus and his successors did not come to a world of primeval peace, but one of tribal rivalries and warfare, which together with the horse, sword, and disease facilitated his and his successors' occupation and conquests. For example, without Indian tribal allies, Cortez could never have conquered Mexico. In each of the seventeenth- and eighteenth-century colonial wars, various groups of natives sided with one or another European power, as in the French and Indian War, the American Revolution, and the War of 1812. Some Indian tribes, like the Cherokees, owned black slaves and developed slave practices and codes similar to that of their white neighbors. Even in the Civil War, tribes were divided in their loyalty to the North or South. And in the "winning of the West," there were always some tribes that helped the American military vanquish other tribes.

Similar belligerency abounded among the European powers. Though they were all white and Christian, Spain, Portugal, England, France, Holland, and Sweden sought wealth in the New World, often at the expense of other colonial powers, but always at the expense of the Indians. The English, of course, won out, but only to be themselves defeated and expelled from the mainland by a minority of rebellious expatriates.

Throughout the nineteenth century, the most hated religious groups were Irish Catholics and Mormons, who were periodically attacked by mobs in the East and West. Anti-Semitism, the oldest form of religious intolerance, was transplanted from Europe and readily practiced by Catholics and Protestants alike, but never to the extent it was practiced in Europe.

Toward the century's end, as large numbers of southern, central, and eastern European immigrants began arriving—Jews, Hungarians, Italians, Poles, Greeks, and Russians—animosities grew between them and previous immigrant groups, as well as among themselves, as they brought their old-country passions and prejudices with them—or adopted those of American citizens, particularly towards Indians, Mexican Americans, Asians, and African Americans, whom they had rarely encountered in their European homelands. Parallel suspicions and animosities grew in the early twentieth century among Asian groups themselves on the West Coast, namely Japanese, Chinese, Asian Indians, and Filipinos.

Wherever interminority group animosities existed, they were vulnerable to exploitation by more powerful groups using a strategy of divide and dominate. And so there were colonists who helped exacerbate inter-Indian relations, slave owners who deliberately purchased Africans from different tribes, and industrial and agricultural employers who sought ethnic and racial pluralism in their workforce in order to prevent unionization. For example, on the West Coast and in Hawaii, white employers exploited cultural differences and animosities among Chinese, Japanese, Korean, and Filipino workers, while on mainland America, employers did the same with European immigrant groups, and the latter with American blacks. "As rapidly as a race rises in the scale of living and . . . begin[s] to demand higher wages and resist the pressure of long hours and over-exertion," wrote an early twentieth-century scholar, "the employers substitute another race and the process is repeated."[1]

In the very plenitude of victims and victimizers, there was a simultaneity, proliferation, and succession of intergroup conflicts, which involved a host of psychological, social, economic, political, religious, and institutional factors, which in turn were influenced by family, friends, schools, popular culture, and governmental policies. Conflicts resulted from some or many of these elements interacting with some or many of the following characteristics:

—suspicion or hatred of others being, appearing, or wanting to be different—culturally, religiously, racially, physically, linguistically

—resentment of others competing for profits, land, jobs, status, political power, or government aid

—envy of those with wealth, political power, social status, education, professional achievement, or even sexual appeal

—susceptibility to political and religious demagoguery

—readiness to conform with dominant value and behavioral patterns of major private and public institutions

—pride in one's own group, wherein distance or separation from others was defended in the name of group security, survival, and general well-being

—a predisposition, if not instinct, within all humans to demean, harm, or aggress other humans

Just as all groups did not suffer equally, so did not all members of a particular group. Much depended on where they lived and especially their socioeconomic standing. African Americans in the South and Asians in the West suffered from a broader and longer range of bigoted actions than did their counterparts in the North and East. Also, within each minority group, those relatively well off socioeconomically were better able to shield themselves from the harsh realities of bigotry, as was true of the late nineteenth- and early twentieth-century German Jews in contrast to Jews from south-central and eastern Europe. A few succeeded in "passing" into the general society—African Americans who were light-skinned and European immigrants who changed their names, religion, and, where necessary, altered facial features through surgery.

How groups responded to bigotry depended much on their size and resources, their historic experiences and cultural traditions, their political and communal power relative to that of their oppressors, the national or local economy at the time, and the character of the people, laws, and circumstances surrounding them. Such numerous qualifications of course make for generalizations (and disputes) rather than certainties (and agreements) in discussing group responses. And yet some generalizations are in order.

First off, not all groups, nor all members of a group, nor all generations of a group reacted in the same way to prejudice and discrimination. Second, the way groups were treated was more often determined by the intentions and ambitions of their aggressors than by their own behavior. Third, the more a group was geographically isolated, possessed work and family values similar to those of the surrounding society, and did not compete economically with other groups, the less it was attacked. Lastly, neither persistent nor periodic bigotry prevented comparatively large numbers of achievers among some groups, such as Armenians, Cubans, Greeks, Huguenots, Japanese, Jews, Koreans, Quakers, and West Indians.

Against that setting, minority responses to bigotry can be categorized as: fatalistic submission, pragmatic accommodation, prudent avoidance, militant defense, retaliatory aggression, fearful relocation to another area or country, or defiant determination to prove that they are not what they are accused of being or that they are as good as or better than their attackers.

Some examples: Hawaiians generally greeted and tolerated European and American intruders in the spirit of "aloha." Under American military occupation, Puerto Ricans were usually friendly and accommodating, while Filipinos grew resentful and rebellious. Chinese on the West Coast were relatively submissive, as were Japanese. The widely dispersed Eskimos in Greenland, Alaska, and Canada were submissive as outsiders—more recently, oil and natural gas developers—overwhelmed them. Like many immigrant parents, the Punjabis in California urged their children to have as little contact as possible with non-Punjabis, ignore bigoted remarks, avoid fights, and achieve academically in school. To avoid religious discrimination and racism, many Hutterites and Garveyites immigrated respectively to Canada and Africa. Mormons fled from gentiles before settling down in Utah.

To victims and victimizers alike, numbers, resources, and cohesiveness were crucial to successful defense or attack. For example, when Catholics were a tiny minority among Protestants, they were consciously accommodating. Before emigrating from seventeenth-century England, Cecil Calvert counseled Catholic immigrants not to offend majority Protestants but to practice their faith "as privately as may be" and remain "silent upon all occasions of discourse concerning matters of Religion."[2]

As Catholics grew in numbers, so did they in organization and militancy. In some cities when attacked by mobs, Catholics formed semi-military units, as in Philadelphia and New York City, where Bishop Hughes devised a plan for occupying each church with 1,000 to 3,000 men who would take "as many lives as they could in defense of their property," and, if necessary, give up "their own lives for the same cause."[3]

By the late nineteenth century, Catholics had gained political power in many large urban cities where they constituted a majority or plurality. However, not until after the presidential election of John F. Kennedy in 1960 did many Catholics stop feeling like a "beleaguered community."

Other minority groups, too, formed organizations to defend themselves from physical or verbal attack, strengthen group cohesiveness, and demonstrate their patriotism. The German Turnverein Society, brought from Germany in 1824, originally focused on gymnastics and politics, and by 1856 had groups in 28 states. Because of nativist attacks on them in the 1850s, particularly in Hoboken, New Jersey, and Louisville, Kentucky, the society encouraged the formation of paramilitary companies. During World War I, many German, Norwegian, and Danish Lutheran groups cooperated in combatting anti-German and anti-Lutheran prejudice. After the war, amid intense xenophobia, the Steuben Society of America was founded to counter negative images of Germany as a nation of "Huns" and of German Americans as a people of divided allegiance.

A few years after arriving in the latter part of the nineteenth century, Japanese immigrants formed the Japanese Association. While most of its activities were social and benevolent, nativist attacks prompted them to adopt self-protective measures, such as contacting the police or the Japanese consul when attacked. The second generation created the Japanese American Citizens League, which combined both protective and acculturationist functions.

The American Jewish Committee came into being in 1906 to "prevent the infraction of the civil and religious rights of Jews in any part of the world" and "to secure for Jews equality of economic, social, and educational opportunity." Seven years later, the Anti-Defamation League of B'nai B'rith was created to combat anti-Semitism as well as to "secure justice and fair treatment for all citizens alike."

Between 1909 and 1911, the first national Negro defense and improvement societies were established: the National Association for the Advancement of Colored People (NAACP) and the National League on Urban Conditions. With the civil rights movement of the 1960s, new and more militant organizations came into being, led mainly or entirely by young African Americans: the Congress of Racial Equality (CORE), the Southern Christian Leadership Conference (SCLC), and the Student Non-Violent Coordinating Committee (SNCC).

Mexican Americans formed mutual aid and protective societies, such as the Alianza Hispano Americana in 1894, the Orden Hijos de America (the Order of the Sons of America) in 1921, and the League of the United Latin American Citizens in 1929, one of whose primary goals was ending bigotry against Mexican Americans.

Largely in response to the post–World War I revival of the Ku Klux Klan in the South and rampant antiforeign feelings, a group of Greek

Americans in Atlanta, Georgia, formed the American Hellenic Educational Progressive Association (AHEPA) in 1922. While committed to acculturation and the use of English in their official meetings, they vigorously defended their Greek heritage and language.

Similar organizing took place among smaller groups and recent immigrant ones. For example, the American-Arab Anti-Defamation Committee was formed in 1980 to combat media stereotyping as well as employment, educational, and political discrimination. In 1985, the Colombian-American Society was organized in Miami to help kinsmen adapt to American life and to counter the jokes and suspicions about Colombians being criminal drug dealers. Because of a few disreputable Colombians, said a society official, "We are getting the bad news and we never took the time to get the good news."[4]

Of course, not all discriminated groups formed self-defense committees or organizations. Those that did not usually were relatively few in number, new to the country, and lacking in financial resources; generally they had no significant political or cultural leaders or associations, were unaccustomed to voluntary group advocacy, or simply didn't think they could do anything to change the situation.

Some groups were fortunate in having their former governments speak up on their behalf. Throughout the late nineteenth and early twentieth centuries, China, Japan, Italy, and Mexico protested industrial abuse and nativist attacks on their former nationals and, at times, succeeded in forcing federal investigations, formal apologies, or indemnifications for families of injured immigrants. Totally without such foreign governmental support, then, were minorities like African Americans, Jews, and Armenians, who had no homeland. In 1994, when California passed Proposition 187, which cut social and educational services to illegal immigrants, the Mexican government issued a statement criticizing "all open and undercover forms of discrimination and any xenophobic practices," and El Salvador's president urged its expatriates not to react violently to the "anti-immigrant" measure.

Though being victimized did not preclude victimizing others, it did prompt some people to be less bigoted and to join coalitions combating bigotry. This is particularly true of the World War II and after generations, who ignored or paid less attention to the intergroup prejudices and passions of their parents and grandparents and who, as a result of military service, travel abroad, acculturation, education, patriotism, religious or political idealism, self-interest, or any combination thereof, believed that racial, religious, and ethnic bigotry were wrong and that their own well-being was best assured when that of other groups also was assured.

In ever increasing numbers and percentages, Americans have supported legislation and social movements seeking to abolish racial, religious, ethnic, and—more recently—age, sexual orientation, gender, and disabled discrimination. Simply put, today's minorities have opportunities and freedoms that their parents or grandparents never had.

In summary, intergroup tensions and conflicts existed from before our beginnings as a nation and multiplied as more and more groups immigrated here. A simultaneity, succession, and proliferation of victims occurred, with the newest immigrant group usually becoming the most targeted. Nevertheless, there were differences in the duration and degree of oppression that groups encountered, as well as differential responses to discrimination and oppression.

All too often, particularly in recent decades, members of each group knew, or want to know, only about their own history, motivated by desires to assert their group pride, roots, and contributions to America, as well as their inclusion in various government affirmative action programs. Such ethnocentrism and group desires have contributed to the continuance and often multiplication of intergroup tensions and conflicts, overshadowing the progress that has been made and hindering the creation of coalitions to solve problems that all or many groups confront.

NOTES

1. Frank Tracy Carlton, *The History and Problems of Organized Labor* (New York: D.C. Heath and Co., 1911), p. 342.

2. John Cogley, *Catholic America* (New York: Dial Press, 1973), p. 10.

3. Edward Wakin, *Enter the Irish-American* (New York: Thomas Y. Crowell Co., 1976), p. 83.

4. "Miami Colombians Seek to Alter Their Image," *New York Times*, 17 August 1985, p. 24.

7

Becoming Insiders: Factors Affecting the Creation and Maintenance of Boundaries for New Immigrants

Judith Goode

New immigration following the Immigration Reform Act of 1965 provides us with the opportunity to examine closely the social construction of ethnic and racial boundaries as new groups of outsiders are incorporated into the social structure of the United States. In 1988, a two-year ethnographic study called the "Philadelphia Changing Relations Project" was begun in eastern North Philadelphia. It was part of a national study sponsored by the Ford Foundation comparing relationships between new immigrants and established Americans in six cities (Bach 1993).

The context for this wave of immigration was different from that of the nineteenth century and early twentieth century. The ethnographic study focused on the effect of these new structural features. Firstly, many of the immigrant groups were coming with higher educational levels and financial capital than had turn-of-the-century immigrants. Secondly, most of the new immigrants are non-European people of color. Thirdly, the industrial expansion of earlier periods had stopped. Deindustrialization and a restructuring service economy shaped the opportunity structure. Finally, public discourse about racism and state favoritism toward minorities in the aftermath of the recent civil rights movement was affecting this mostly nonwhite immigration.

This chapter will argue that these circumstances have produced new processes of identity formation and group boundaries. Yet, at the same time, individuals frequently cross these boundaries in local everyday interactions as they work to construct meaningful lives and relationships. In order for the openings created by these individual acts to lead to overcoming boundaries created by larger political and economic forces we must become more conscious of how these boundaries are formed and how they can be transcended.

The Philadelphia Changing Relations Project involved a team of ethnographers comparing three neighborhoods within Philadelphia to discover ways in which particular local contexts affected relationships.[1] Philadelphia had the lowest rate of immigration of the six project cities.[2] While it ranks fifth in size in the United States, it ranks only sixteenth as a recipient of new immigrants (*Philadelphia Inquirer*, September 12, 1988).

The research project focused primarily on three newcomer groups— Koreans, Puerto Ricans, and Polish refugees—in their interactions with established European Americans and African Americans. As we proceeded, other newcomer groups were incorporated. Some of the established Americans labeled themselves as hyphenated ethnic Americans while others did not. We looked at interactions among members of these groups in particular arenas that we thought would be most likely to bring them together: schools, neighborhood organizations, workplaces, and shopping strips.

CITYWIDE PROCESSES

This study was conducted with attention to several levels of socioeconomic and political forces that influence the way people interact. One important level is the nature of the regional political economy. Philadelphia is a region that underwent a major shift from industrial to service jobs after World War II. (Adams et al., 1991).

During the period of the recent immigration, the city of Philadelphia has been in decline. Between 1970 and 1990, the city suffered a loss of over 19 percent of the population. This was accompanied by a major loss of manufacturing jobs; employment has shifted to service occupations, with 75 percent of the city's population so employed. Many people are working in non-union jobs with a two-tier wage system or in part-time work with no benefits (Goode and Schneider 1994: 32–40).

However, neighborhoods have experienced these processes differently.

Since the rapid suburbanization of the white population, the city has become increasingly segregated by race (Goldstein, 1986). The polarization of residential space as black and white (and the creation of lines that are defended) has created a structure that has affected the way in which newcomers settled and are accepted.

Also framing the interaction of newcomers and established residents is the increasing media focus on race and ethnicity, both local and national. Over the last two decades, two major frameworks have emerged for viewing difference in the United States. One, emerging from the civil rights movement focuses on race, most commonly understood as the relationship between blacks and whites.[3] It emphasizes historical relationships of power and economics, specifically an understanding of the history of structured racial inequality. Newcomer people of color are sometimes incorporated into this discourse as people of color from post-colonial states.

The other framework ignores race in favor of ''culture.'' The United States is seen as a nation that is metaphorically a tapestry, mosaic, quilt, or salad in which different but equal cultural components contribute to a valued diversity. Structured inequality is overlooked and equal opportunity is emphasized.[4]

The political-economic trajectory of the city and the economic competition it generates between groups intersects with public discourses on racial and ethnic difference to create the conditions that shape people's views of others. However, at the same time, people's everyday lives include face-to-face interactions that occur locally and contradict the expected boundaries and oppositions. Understanding how this works can enable us to remove these barriers and build better intergroup relations.

NEIGHBORHOOD VARIATION

Neighborhoods play an important role in mediating social relations. Our three neighborhoods, Kensington, Port Richmond, and Olney, once shared many traits. The first two were mill towns that housed European factory workers in row homes since the early 1900s. Olney was a nearby streetcar suburb built in the late 19th century for upwardly mobile families from the nearby industrial areas (Goode and Schneider 1994: 104–34). The particular histories of neighborhoods within the city led to the attraction of different groups and to turnover at different rates and times. These processes set different local scenes for the interaction of newcomers and established residents.

Kensington is a Philadelphia neighborhood with a longstanding history as a stable industrial zone (Binzen 1970; Seder 1990). It was hard hit by deindustrialization in the 1970s, as plants that had employed families for generations relocated or closed, thereby affecting the value of homes. Mortgage redlining further affected the private housing market. As residents lost jobs, they were unable to maintain or sell their homes, which usually represented their life savings. Housing abandonment and other forms of blight increased. A substandard rental market developed as well. City service delivery declined and several centers of heavy drug activity developed.

Since the 1970s, nonwhite groups have been coming into the neighborhood. Newcomers are largely Puerto Ricans and blacks moving eastward. There are also small numbers of other Latinos, Vietnamese settled by state agencies, and a community of Palestinians who own residential and commercial property. Koreans are also present as merchants, but only a few are in residence.

Residents see space as belonging to different groups. The basic opposition is between whites and Latinos. Certain areas are seen as "white" and others as controlled by Latinos where Spanish speaking is dominant in public. African Americans speak English, are fewer in number and have been in the neighborhood longer. They are often seen by whites as more similar to themselves in interests and language. For example, one white woman talked about how she got along very well with her daughter's black in-laws because she shared language and customs with them. She contrasted this to her friend's problems with their daughter's Puerto Rican in-laws.

In Kensington we worked in two subareas. One was described by everyone as "belonging" to Latinos, who are the most visible group in public. Their language is heard more frequently than English, and they are significantly represented in the local institutions, schools, churches, and organizations. Yet the significant number of European-American families who live in this area had close ties to their Latino neighbors and participated in mixed block organizations whose success is visible in joint beautification projects.

In the other subarea of Kensington, European Americans still dominate in terms of numbers and public visibility. Here, the high turnover and flight of the last two decades has contributed to a loss of former institutions. The rapid immigration of Latinos is viewed differently by many. As one woman said, "We were good hosts. We took them all in without any trouble. Look at what happened in Port Richmond [referring to a recent incident of harassment]. We don't do that here."[5] Yet fear of Spanish language dominance and the fact that Latinos are seen as transient contribute to concerns about community instability and declining property values.

Port Richmond has been relatively isolated geographically by a street and traffic pattern that deviates from that in the rest of the city. This has helped it to maintain a strong boundary. It remains a working-class neighborhood. Its residents replaced former heavy industrial jobs with new ones in smaller factories and the building trades as well as with white collar jobs.

The Port Richmond neighborhood is built around nationality parishes as core institutions. The four tall spires of Polish, Italian, German, and territorial (Irish) churches symbolically dominate the main crossroad and remind everyone of the turn-of-the-century immigrants who founded them. Today, the area is the heart of the Polish community and the locus of most of its citywide social institutions.

Port Richmond is a tightly bounded enclave that projects the image of a stable small town. Still, there are many new residents. Many of these are whites who have moved eastward from changing Kensington. They associate the decline in Kensington with the coming of people of color rather than with institutional disinvestment and want to reinforce the color line. Other newer residents come from places where they had successful relations with different groups in workplaces and neighborhoods. They would like to erase the image of racist inhospitality.

Those in Port Richmond who fear the westward approach of racially different newcomers tend to have had very little experience with diverse groups. Many elderly members of the community rarely come into contact with blacks or immigrants other than Polish refugees except in the shopping centers, where most contact is transitory and impersonal and takes place under stress in checkout lines.

The experience with Polish newcomers illustrates a community attitude toward outsiders in general. The established Polish-American community is ambivalent about the new Polish refugees who have arrived since the Refugee Act of 1980. They come from very different class backgrounds. New Poles are more educated, urban, and cosmopolitan than the earlier Polish Americans, who were transformed from rural peasants to factory workers in the United States. The resentment expressed by the established Polish Americans of the failure of newcomers to participate in community institutions sounds very much like the complaints about immigrants in other neighborhoods. Yet, elsewhere, such class-based resentments get blamed on race or national culture (Goode and Schneider 1994).

Olney, the early streetcar suburb, is still seen by many as a "pass-through" place where people move "up" on the way to something better.[6] Its housing is newer and larger than housing in the other two neighborhoods. For the most part, as Olney did not tie its residents to local workplaces, it was never as residentially stable as Kensington and Port Richmond.

Olney today is characterized by increasing turnover and cultural diversity. It is the area with the highest number of real estate transactions in the city (Stains and Marchese 1988). Older residents seeing change describe Olney as threatened by the decline further south. People point to trash, dirt, increasing crime, and drug-related activity as signs of the breakdown of civic order.[7] However, Olney is considered a garden spot by both the police districts that contain it because, while the crime rate may be increasing, it is still very low.[8] Housing is still largely owner-occupied.

New residents in Olney are overwhelmingly young and middle class. Olney has the fastest-growing school population in the city. Included are a significant number of native-born black and white families, who are attracted by the affordable quality housing and good schools. For them the diversity is a plus. New immigrants include Latinos—Puerto Ricans, Colombians, Chileans, Guatemalans, Cubans, and Mexicans—as well as Koreans, Vietnamese, Hmong, Cambodians, Portuguese, Indians, and Pakistanis. There are also several West Indian black families.[9] The shift in population has occurred more recently and faster than in Kensington. There is less spatial segregation of residential areas. During our field work we became familiar with seven blocks, each with a broad range of groups represented.

In all three neighborhoods, it is hard to disentangle the relative effects of three variables: (1) prejudice against the racially different; (2) conflicts over language or lifestyle (cooking smells, loud music, large extended families in small houses, and the like); and (3) the very significant effects of being an "outsider" in a community trying to hang on to a disappearing sense of continuity. Examples of European-American newcomers feeling like unwelcome outsiders in a neighborhood and actions against white newcomers perceived as antisocial are frequent. Conversely, the few blacks and Latinos who have lived in all three neighborhoods for a long time are taken for granted as members of one community unmarked by difference.[10]

It is also difficult to disentangle the effects of class on the perception of difference. European Americans talk about their "trashy" established neighbors as causing more problems than their aspiring middle-class newcomer neighbors, who are often professionals or skilled technical workers. Blacks use the term "nigger" to refer to poorer blacks who, they fear, will follow and spoil their new neighborhood and financial investment.[11]

LOCAL INTERACTION

People come together within the neighborhoods in several ways. Starting with the most intimate and personal level of individual relationships, we will move to a discussion of continuous, regular interaction in larger, more public arenas. Finally, the group-to-group interactions that occur in community organizations and community events will be discussed.

Personal Networks

We encountered a striking number of trusting, friendly ties among people of different backgrounds in Olney and Kensington. In these neighborhoods, which are viewed from the outside as hostile to newcomers of different races or nationalities, many people were living lives that incorporated those who were different much more significantly than their suburban peers. This was true in spite of the sheer density of preexisting social relationships in their everyday life.

Established residents, largely working class, are embedded in social networks made up of relatives and long-term childhood friends. While many of these friends and kin are in the neighborhood, others are located nearby. Those who have remained in Kensington relate to kin and childhood friends who have moved to Port Richmond and areas further north, such as Olney, as well as to higher status areas.

Newcomers are also usually tied to kin as migration often involves moving near kin or friends from the homeland. Common communities of origin often link people to those they knew before or to those on whom they can make social claims through traceable connections or mutual ties. These personal networks take significant time and energy to tend.

Over and over, both established and new immigrant families described weekends and evenings filled with social obligations to kin and friends in family celebrations. Frequent demands were made for help, such as child care, care of the sick, and regular visiting.

In spite of this, new friendships formed. The most intimate ties were those of dating and intermarriage. We knew many intermarried couples, and many families we interviewed had brothers- and sisters-in-law, nieces and nephews from other racial or new immigrant groups. There were examples of intergroup marriages across all possible group lines in Olney and Kensington.[12]

Children were the "icebreakers" and brokers between individuals from different backgrounds. Over and over, such intimate friendships between people developed because of their children's friendships. In the many instances where "best friends" were from different backgrounds, family contact was significant. This led to phone contact, birthday dinners, and other family celebrations in each other's homes, and, consequently, an awareness of the nature of family life in each other's homes.[13]

Women who work in multiethnic workplaces often break down barriers by talking about common experiences with raising children and dealing with husbands. Several examples of close friendships, godparenthood, and quasi-kin relations grew up between Latino- and European-American women in work situations in which the family was "brought to work" in terms of storytelling. In several instances, established residents serve as paid babysitters in their homes for newcomer women. The common attachment to the children, who are seen as innocent and neutral, often develops a close bond of caring and mutual nurturance.

Sometimes common quality-of-life problems relating to children's safety led to the formation of active block associations in which there is frequent, recurring contact. One block association formed around the need to deal with a troublesome teenager and a "crack" house, the resultant group has existed for over three years and maintains an empty lot as a play area. Its members include Puerto Ricans, Koreans, Cambodians, European Americans, and blacks, and it meets every month in the home of the leader. Families on the block are all on a first-name basis.

Underlying all of these successes, we find women to be the main actors, using their concerns about family and children to cross boundaries and develop relationships. Furthermore, success is based on stability. In every case, intimacy has taken time. Residence on the block or tenure in the workplace must be stable in order for these relationships to grow. Yet the political and economic realities in Philadelphia promote transiency and turnover in neighborhoods and workplaces.

Structured Arenas

In institutional arenas like shopping strips, schools, and workplaces, regular interactions were less personal. Formal and informal rules and practices have developed that channel interaction between newcomers and established residents. For example, schools were shaped by official school district policies, but each school had a particular history of critical events and informal traditions.

Business Strips

The relationships on the business strip are less intimate and more formal than on the block as they occur in a public setting. Over time a social order has been established. Some groups have laid claim to certain times and places while avoiding others. In Olney, storekeepers reported identical temporal patterns of shopping for different race, ethnic, and age groups. These were confirmed by biweekly observation over a two-year period.

In strip retailing, certain practices in the setting up of stores keep interaction at a minimum. Several Korean merchants stated that they have reorganized the physical space in their stores to maximize self-service and minimize conversation because of language difficulties.[14] The older stores of established merchants are characterized by counters along three walls. They force attention on the customer as soon as she enters the store. Customers are immediately asked if they need help and it is impossible to avoid conversation. Newcomers avoid these settings because they require language, alternatively, they often bring children to translate and broker business for them. In the supermarket, newcomers tend to shop in family groups and walk about chatting with each other in circumscribed groupings in their own language and providing mutual support.

Language is a potent barrier for adults in ways that were unexpected. One established merchant, when asked whether he knew of any regular Latino and Asian customers, says that he knows his regular customers who are European American and African American because he talks to them about sports events or the weather. Because he cannot engage in such chats with newcomers, he says he "doesn't know their faces" and cannot identify them as regulars.[15]

Korean Merchants

One illustration of the importance of local context in the nature of relationships can be seen by comparing the local role and experience of Korean merchants in two communities. In each instance, we are looking both at relationships between newcomer merchants and their customers from different backgrounds and between merchants from different backgrounds. Korean merchants are well organized in the city. There is a citywide businessman's association that has seven suborganizations. This community of entrepreneurs is connected both to the homeland and to other merchants in other cities. Korean newspapers in each city keep everyone informed about events and incidents in this global network.[16]

There is a hierarchy among the merchants. While some fit the dominant stereotype of owners of "mom and pop" grocery stores, others cater to upscale clients downtown and/or own several different enterprises. A pattern of turning over stores and purchasing better ones or owning multiple stores in several neighborhoods characterizes those with long experience and large amounts of capital. Outside of retailing, there are also investment opportunities in business brokering, wholesale and small-scale garment production (Power 1988).

In both Kensington and Olney there is a heavy presence of Korean retail merchants. However, because of structural dissimilarities, inter-group relations are different. In Kensington, merchants cater to their Latino clientele and employ Latino workers. Here there are mostly positive interactions, and Koreans pick up some knowledge of the Spanish language, particularly colors, numbers, and greetings. One reason for this congeniality is that there is no feeling of displacement or "takeover" on this business strip. This area was largely abandoned before the current owners began to buy stores in the last few years. Most owners, Korean or not, are new. Community residents were pleased to see the strip return to life and commented on the ways in which local merchants catered to their needs. One of the merchants here claimed he was the first in the city to establish contact with wholesalers of products for Puerto Ricans.

Jobs have been provided for Latino workers as Spanish-speaking staff is considered an asset in serving customers, and many employees say they prefer working for Koreans than for whites, whom they perceive as racist.[17] Store owners share this fear of encounters with whites, who are perceived as arrogant and racist. Both non-English-speaking groups prefer transactions that do not involve much talk. Merchants and customers search for commonalities between themselves and differences from established Americans. For example, there was frequent talk of a common preference for fresh produce as opposed to American preference for processed food.

There is conflict on the strip, but it is largely among the merchants. Here, hypercompetitiveness due to the nature of business in this very poor neighborhood has pitted the Koreans against established merchants. One established merchant has tried to organize a merchant's association that would be able to take advantage of some of the development programs of the city. He sees his efforts as having been sabotaged by the lack of interest on the part of the Korean merchants. There have been some unpleasant public exchanges.[18]

In Olney the business district has long provided both everyday goods and services, as well as more specialty services (such as clothing, shoes, appliances, records, and gifts). The strip was once an upscale magnet, which drew its clientele from all over the city. In recent years the established merchants have been retiring, having educated their children as professionals. Consequently, they need buyers for their stores. In the last fifteen years, national and regional chains catering to low-income customers have become significant, and the strip was seen as declining.

Koreans began buying stores in the late 1970s. There are two types of Korean-owned stores. Many continue to appeal to established English-speaking clientele and often maintain the same staff, merchandise, and suppliers. Others have been converted to serve the Korean community (specialty retail and wholesaling to smaller retailers). In the mid-1980s, there was talk in the press and on the street about Olney becoming "Koreatown," a social center for Koreans and a wholesale center for merchandise that one Korean leader claimed would be the biggest in the Middle Atlantic states.[19]

Resentment in the established community can be traced to the growth of stores for Koreans only, which are the subject of rumor and suspicion. Stores that are labeled "wholesale" and lock out neighborhood customers are viewed by established residents as evidence that they are losing the shopping strip, the heart of Olney. Traffic patterns are such that all traffic must traverse this shopping strip, which is the symbolic center of the neighborhood and the site of major community events: a July 4th parade, Super Sunday, and other celebrations. Memories of the former upscale strip fuel the sense of loss.[20]

Conflicts between Korean merchants and local customers largely center on loss of access. One local resident reported trying to enter a store and being told by a Korean woman shaking her head, "no, no wholesale."[21] The fear of losing the strip through a complete takeover by "Koreatown" underlay the Korean sign incident in 1986. On the same day that a newspaper article entitled "Olney to Become Koreatown" appeared, Korean alphabet street signs were erected on the strip. The public outcry and its public resolution still loom large in the consciousness of Olney residents.[22]

Yet there are other contributing factors to discomfort. Established residents can't practice the expected small talk of local store interaction with Korean storekeepers. The new Korean self-service arrangements designed to minimize linguistic interactions lead to more surveillance and a feeling on the part of customers that they are not trusted. Some Korean merchants who are fearful of their customers use bullet-proof customer barriers. Incidents of storekeepers pulling guns on local teenagers have occurred. Suspicion and distrust about language ability is common: "One storekeeper speaks English to me on some days, but on other days he conveniently claims he does not understand when I know he does."[23]

Stores that make the most successful transition from established to Korean ownership are those that make few changes. In one, the new Korean owner enjoys making pizza in the window while the community enjoys the performance. A produce stand and a hardware store, which employ Latinos, also please a very diverse clientele.

While customer problems are greater in Olney than in Kensington, the relations between merchants are less problematic. Here, a very strong merchants' association welcomed Korean investment to protect strip viability at this critical point of turnover. Wary that wholesale businesses would destroy the strip, they have developed an alliance with Korean merchants who serve the general public and who share an interest in the strip's multicultural future. Several Koreans have been incorporated into the leadership of the group. The cooperation between Koreans and established merchants is a situation unparalleled in the city.

Schools

Schools are more complex institutions in which there is more regular contact among people in nonanonymous situations. Formal structures of authority coexist with informal structures. For example, in addition to professional educators in schools, who often come from outside the neighborhood, there are paid aides who supervise the lunchroom and the playground. These are usually local community women. While they may be seen as insignificant by the administration, they can be very important in channeling interaction during socially important times of the day.[24]

In one school, newcomer parents who mistrust the school hang around the perimeter of the playground. However, their contact with their children is controlled by the aides, who impose "rules" about contact and interdict the delivery of special foods. Newcomer parents stand around complaining about the way the aides treat them and their children while the aides complain about the way that newcomers break the rules. This development of conflict occurs without the knowledge or interest of the authorities who focus on the formal policies of the classroom (Goode, Schneider, and Blanc 1992).

In another school, the populations are divided into two camps: English-speaking parents and aides and Latino parents and aides. Both groups of parents are dissatisfied with the school, which is overcrowded because increasing numbers of overflow Latino students from even more overcrowded nearby schools are being bussed in. While the parents of established students focus their anger on school district policies and the principal rather than the Latinos, they do nothing to develop alliances with Spanish speakers. Latino parents see the poor European-American families at the school as part of the white racist power structure in the city and not as allies in a common battle. Both groups have similar complaints and concerns about their children, but they see each other as part of the problem (Goode, Schneider, and Blanc 1992).

Children in elementary school seem mostly to ignore group identities in everyday school life. While there is a lot of joking and teasing about skin color, food habits, and the like, there are many examples of tight-knit friendships across groups. The most potent forces structuring children's social relations are student turnover, the way the school uses language to organize children, and the way families exert social controls on their children's activities outside of school.

One structural feature that had an effect on interrelations was the stability of the student population in the school. One school was given unusual control of its student population by allowing children to enter only in the first grade. The students all lived within walking distance. Thus, each age cohort tended to spend all eight grades with the same students and their school friendships were reinforced by contact in the neighborhood, leading to very successful friendships. In other public schools, populations were very transient because the school district changed catchment areas every year. Parochial schools in neighborhoods with high turnover were forced to recruit from outside the parish to maintain adequate enrollment. In such conditions of flux, it was difficult to maintain the many friendships that form in school.

Language does not necessarily separate children in school unless there are boundaries among groups created by the official or informal structure of the school. While all the schools we worked in took in students with no English at the beginning of the year, the pace at which they learned depended on the nature of informal segregation and clique membership in the school, which were often unintentionally channeled by school policies and expectations.

In the school that admitted the overflow population of Latino children from different nearby schools each year, it was this turnover and instability in the school population that created the separatist structure. Latinos from outside the neighborhood came in with ties previously formed in former schools and were a structure apart, while Latinos who lived in the mixed surrounding neighborhood were likely to belong to mixed cliques. The ESOL (English for Speakers of Other Languages) children tended to be formally segregated throughout the day in special classes and informally segregated at the lunch tables and in the playground.[25] The fact that Spanish-speaking aides and English-speaking aides avoided one another added to the division in the school.

Such patterns are not necessary. In the stable school, children moved easily from their ESOL classes to activities with other friends. No language other than English was ever heard in public spaces. This was the result of both student stability and conscious school policy.

In still another school, a parochial one with no official ESOL resources, it was assumed that newcomer children took at least a year to learn English. They were grouped together throughout the day and each assigned a bilingual "buddy" as translator. They were not given English texts in their subject matter. The presumption of non-English-speaking was so strongly held that nobody ever spoke to them in English; furthermore, they were spoken about in English in their presence. Knowing that they were expected to speak their native language, they complied even when their English blossomed. They switched to speaking English with their English-speaking friends as soon as they left the school. In all schools different expectations and assumptions held by the authorities shaped the behaviors of children.

Immigrant children tend to play with children of their parents' friends and relatives outside of school in spite of developing other ties in school. Parents involve their children in many activities within the ethnic community trying to shield them from perceived American permissiveness.

One Portuguese girl spent many afternoons working in a Portuguese day care center. Both she and her diverse friends saw this as interfering with their close friendship.

Schools are beginning to bring newcomer and established adults together, but most Home and School Associations are controlled by established residents, who complain about difficulties in involving newcomer parents. In all the schools we worked in, parent leaders complained that newcomer parents did not come to meetings. Many newcomer parents are unfamiliar with such organizations and need special activities to incorporate them. The organizations continue to rely on formal notices and phone calls to get people to attend, and both methods lead to miscommunication.

We also observed many instances in which newcomer parents did come to events but were ignored. At one meeting, several Latino parents came in response to a flyer. Because the parent leaders thought these parents did not speak English, they avoided any personal contact with them. This kind of mutual interest in the nature and quality of education is something that can be used to develop cross-group relationships in neighborhoods; however, it cannot work unless established residents realize that they must use more personal communication and explain their missions more clearly.

These examples demonstrate how local institutions create unintentional boundaries among groups. Official school policies can either increase or decrease turnover in schools, having tremendous implications for the creation of group boundaries. Well intentioned practices of native-born and newcomer storekeepers or of school administrators and parent leaders often unintentionally create tension and conflict. In such ways, the often friendly personal relationships among households on the block become contradicted by tense interactions in local institutions. Confounding this further are the ways in which larger discussions of race, ethnicity, and nationality frame ideas about groups.

GROUP DEFINITION AND INTERACTION

Labeling Groups

In all of the neighborhoods confusing systems of labels based on race, language, and nationality are being negotiated. The discourses of difference that emerged from the experience with African Americans and the civil rights movement focus on race, while the experience with earlier waves of immigration has engendered the model of ethnic pluralism.

There are three sets of categories in play: new immigrant groups define themselves; the state uses official census categories; and established residents categorize newcomers using these and other criteria (Keefe 1989: 1–8).

Newcomers largely use categories based on nationality (or subnational ethnicity) for themselves. On the other hand, census categories lump many nationalities together as Hispanics or as Asians. Established residents are faced with both sets of labels as well as distinctions based on language and racial physical attributes such as skin color.

A complex process of negotiation occurs when a group labels itself and develops an identity from the inside but is responded to by outsiders imposing another set of labels. For example, on the street all Asians frequently are called "Chinese" by established Americans whether they are Korean, Cambodian, Vietnamese, or, in fact, Chinese.[26] Puerto Ricans who maintain boundaries between themselves and other Latinos (Goode and McCormack 1990) are recognized officially as Hispanics or Latinos.

People's acceptance of labels varies situationally. We have seen occasions when non-Chinese Asians refer to themselves as Chinese and Puerto Ricans as Spanish (the common established street terms) to outsiders because it is easier to accept the outsiders' label than to explain the complexities.[27] We have also seen people get angry and protest the broader labels, asserting, for example, their Cambodian or Colombian identities. The same variability exists when dark-skinned Puerto Ricans tacitly accept status as blacks in certain situations, while in others they exhibit a fierce national pride. Responses depend on the context and whether or not these are ongoing relationships.

There was great confusion in all neighborhoods about which category to use and a general lack of appreciation of the complexities within the Asian and Latino communities. Language, skin color, and nationality play different and often contradictory roles in defining insiders and outsiders. People from India in Olney are sometimes considered to be black or more frequently Hispanic because of their skin color. Their physical features do not fit their official Asian category. Portuguese were considered to be just another group of "Spanish." The significant rate of intermarriage among groups also confounds the pluralist view that everybody fits neatly into a category. Yet newspapers, television, and talk-radio sources that emphasized the simplistic official macrocategories were often used as authoritative albeit confusing sources of correct usage.

People often focused on "culture" as the basis of difference among groups even though those being lumped together shared little in common in terms of cultural heritage or life experience. Recall the differences between established Polish Americans and Polish refugees, who presumably share "Polish" culture. Among Latinos, not only are there many nationality groups, but even within the Puerto Rican community there are vast differences. Many families have been in the city for twenty to thirty years and have several generations of locally born offspring; further, there are third and fourth generation mainland-born people of Puerto Rican background who have recently moved from New York and New Jersey.[28] All of these groups have variable commitments and contact with life on the island, some visiting frequently and others not at all. There are also newcomers from Puerto Rico itself whose presence is signaled by the constant entry of Spanish-speaking children requiring ESOL programs. These subgroups do not necessarily relate to one another. Yet Puerto Ricans and even Latinos as a group are assumed to be homogeneous and tightly knit.

Community Organizations and Diversity Events

At the neighborhood level, community organizations also contend with two notions of difference, one based on institutional racism and the other based on "culture." Many activist groups are trying to empower minorities, whom they see as victims of institutional racism stemming from differences in political or economic power. At the same time, the idea that conflict results from "cultural" misunderstandings based on differences in language or expressive style has led to a human relations approach that emphasizes learning about cultural difference.

Both Kensington and Olney are involved in programs designed to bring newcomers and established residents together around safe areas of cultural difference: music, food, and art. The main techniques used for these activities involve "culture at a distance" performances or generating artificial person-to-person closeness in workshops designed to break down barriers. These activities are removed from everyday life and often create boundaries and competition among groups.

In Olney, civic organizations were based on a middle-class model of civic betterment, which served to sponsor community events and link local organizations like churches and sports leagues together. Today more and more organization-sponsored programs in Olney focus specifically on the new cultural diversity. Often some of the very programs that are designed to bring people together keep them apart.

Because each immigrant segment is seen as a separate and homogeneous community, most of the formal contact between established residents and newcomer groups occurs through individuals in the newcomer group who make themselves available to outsiders. Very few established community leaders dealt with anyone but these informal brokers. Moreover, only a few individuals in the established community felt comfortable in contacting ethnic brokers. Many of those who talked sincerely about liking the new diversity had never had direct contact with a newcomer.

The newcomer brokers often had limited ties to the "communities" they represented. Often people we interviewed in the newcomer community told us that they had no knowledge of or contact with the individual who is seen by local organizations as representing them. Brokers often represent only one network in a complex internally divided population.

As the vision of the community as a set of culturally separate entities becomes concretized, it not only fails to include some of the groups whose members are less visible (like the South Asians from India or Pakistan) but it glosses over the fluidities of multiple identities, intermarriage, and constant change in community composition.

The very planning and carrying out of multiethnic events often serves to keep people apart as programs are segregated into ethnic components. Immigrant brokers are contacted by a central organizer, who is the only person linked to all groups. At events, people segregate themselves by time and space as they sit with those of their own group, eat their own foods, and leave after their group has performed. Such events also increase friction among groups as they fight over space for booths, places on the program, and time allocations.[29] One parish repeated such an event over several years, however, and was able to change these practices. Over time, it shifted the planning and implementation from the sponsoring priests to an intergroup committee. Initial fears that delegating responsibility would lead to failure were soon overcome.

We have noticed that special events that try to bring people together to learn about one another force everybody to fit the model of America as made up of separate ethnic cultures. This blurs the distinction between immigrants who cross a major cultural boundary in their lifetime and

native-born ethnics whose heritage is restricted to certain symbolic practices. Often fourth- and fifth-generation Americans who have intermarried between nationality groups are pushed to reinvent an ethnic heritage,
especially during special events and festivals. At one event, established
residents joked about their many fractional heritages. One boy mentioned
that he was one-eighth Polish, one eighth German, among other parts.[30]
The only European-American group that had a performance was the
Irish. One Latino newcomer took this to mean that all established residents in the neighborhood were Irish, a misunderstanding that horrified
his European-American neighbors.

The reduction of cultural differences to arts performances avoids areas
of real conflict of interest, such as the competition over the shopping
strip. In some Olney organizations leaders have tried to keep negative
comments out of the public discourse and consider those who make even
legitimate complaints about specific newcomer behavior to be racially
prejudiced (Goode 1990). However, established residents have real fears
about economic decline and loss of community, which must be openly
confronted. Avoiding these issues will force these concerns underground.

The organizations in Kensington used to be like those in Olney today.
However, as the neighborhood changed, new types of organizations developed in response to federal programs and social action movements.
They are primarily concerned with developing affordable housing, creating jobs, decreasing unemployment and curtailing drug-related activities and crime in the neighborhood. Direct programming to improve
intergroup relations was not a priority.

Yet several groups took advantage of Neighborhood Human Relations
Projects funding in spite of their reservations.[31] These projects emphasized using festivals and sensitivity workshops to improve relationships.
Unfortunately, these programs drained the limited resources and energies
of the organizations and created stress among groups and organizations
as they worked together in high-pressure situations. The original skepticism concerning such festivals proved to be correct. The best way to
improve relationships is by improving the neighborhood. Through building on relationships forged on the block, one antidrug coalition has
successfully recruited both newcomer Latino and established European-
American activists and broken down the common barrier between them
observed in schools and residential patterns.

In Port Richmond there were no overarching civic associations at all.
While there were town watch groups and sports leagues, these operated
out of the churches. This community still relied on the parishes, their

schools, and the Polish social service agencies as basic building blocks. Regarded by city agencies as a white racial monolith resisting diversity, Port Richmond was also ignored by the citywide human relations networks. In the summer of 1989, after an incident in Port Richmond involving Latinos and established white residents, several Kensington and Port Richmond organizations tried to mount some antiracist activities. There were no organizations in Port Richmond comparable to the empowerment-oriented Kensington structures. The style of leadership and the rhetoric of the Kensington empowerment groups did not mesh well with those of the parish-based entities. This was one of several factors that ultimately led to the withdrawal of the initially enthusiastic Port Richmond participants.[32]

CONCLUSION

The findings of the Changing Relations Project show that the incorporation of new immigrants does not follow any natural or inevitable progression. Instead, people's identities, social relationships, and ideas about others are fluid and changing depending on who they are with and in what institutional context. Individuals simultaneously hold positive and negative views about the very same groups. They enjoy positive and intimate friendships with people across group boundaries but still share the dominant ideas about groups developed in structured institutions and in media discourse.

State and institutional policies serve in many ways to divide people into categories, appoint brokers, and allocate group resources, often constructing groups that have no grass roots reality. At the same time, individuals, through their everyday interactions, cross boundaries in an attempt to create meaningful lives and solve local problems. These very initiatives are counteracted by the constant reification of social categories in social programs. Without care, celebrating ethnicity frequently not only reinforces stereotypes but ironically strengthens the boundaries it hopes to reduce.

The sources of tension created by the structural realities of the new immigration are frequently ignored. Often new immigrants, like the Polish intelligentsia or the majority of the Korean small entrepreneurs who come with university degrees, have middle-class aspirations and do not expect to start at the bottom. This causes resentment among the working-class Polish American hosts in the first case and the white and African-

American working class customers on the other, who expect immigrants to struggle at the bottom like their families did.

The conjunction of a declining and restructuring economy and the misunderstanding of social programs also affects the process. Depending on whether one is white or of color, all tensions are simplistically blamed on either pervasive racism or governmental favoritism and handouts. There is little awareness of the complex social processes at work.

As a result, the nature of successful relationships on the ground are overlooked. There is little attention to counteracting forces that promote transiency and impede the growth of these relationships. Other unintentional barriers formed within local institutions like schools and shopping strips remain unchecked. Instead, strategies that strengthen boundaries and emphasize differences are favored over strategies that encourage building on the existing intimacy and trust among individuals. These local collaborations are formed around common concerns about children, schools, and safety.

NOTES

1. A team of four ethnographers and four part-time graduate students undertook regular participant observation in several sites in each neighborhood. They were supplemented by additional student volunteers throughout the period. Observations and informal interviews took place with newcomer and established households we had come to know well during the research. During 1988 and 1989, when we did the fieldwork, we amassed reams of records, countless observations, informal discussions, and formal interviews. Our interpretive task was long and complex.

2. The other cities were among the most rapidly changing in the country: Miami, Houston, Monterey Park, California (a suburb of Los Angeles), and Chicago. The sixth city, Garden City, Kansas, was a meatpacking "boom" town that was experiencing a rapid increase in refugee resettlement and newcomer Mexican-American in-migration in a formerly declining agricultural region. The sunbelt cities were experiencing economic growth or recovery from the oil bust (Houston); only Chicago and Philadelphia were deindustrializing rustbelt cities restructuring their economies (Bach 1993).

3. Over a two-year period the two daily newspapers in Philadelphia published articles that contrasted blacks to whites more than once a week.

4. This model was frequently invoked in media feature articles, school programs, conferences, and festivals throughout the two-year study.

5. Field notes, March 11, 1988.

6. Olney has always received northwardly moving, aspiring middle-class

populations from North Philadelphia, and some contemporary leaders came to the area twenty years ago in the wake of the North Philadelphia riots. Many Catholics, of both established European and Latino descent, describe the same northward routes from parish to parish as they came from North Philadelphia whether twenty-five, fifteen, or five years ago.

7. This common refrain was the subject of part of every monthly meeting of both venerable community organizations (Field notes, GOCC and OFN files), the subject of a Home and School Association campaign at one of the schools, as well as a frequent topic of casual conversation.

8. Interviews with Officer W at 35th Precinct and JV and HT of Olney Townwatch, April 1989.

9. The populations of the three schools we studied provides a view of this variety: school A—28 percent white (including Portuguese newcomers), 22 percent black (including West Indians), 30 percent Latino, and 20 percent Asian; school B—31 percent white, 18 percent black, 32 percent Latino, and 18 percent Asian; school C—35 percent white, 18 percent black, 14 percent Latino, and 33 percent Asian.

10. The best example of this is the fact that the incident that led up to the murder of a European-American in Port Richmond was started by a long-term resident black. As he was considered an insider, the fact that he was black was never mentioned or considered important in our many discussions with people in the community.

11. Household interviews 0–5, 0–8.

12. For example, among the research participants in one school, there was a Central American–Southeast Asian, a Filipino–American black, and several established African American–European American, Puerto Rican–European American and Puerto Rican–African American couples.

13. One established family had a sixth-grade son whose best friend was a Puerto Rican boy. Both boys entered each other's homes without knocking (observations at the house and household interview 0–10).

14. Interview with NM, May 1989.

15. Interview with JB, July 1988.

16. Interviews with three heads of Korean organizations and one business broker, August-October 1990.

17. Household interviews K–3, K–5, K–6.

18. Interviews with five merchants at Front and Kensington included complaints about competition. Casual conversation with community residents about merchants undercutting each other's prices in an underhanded way (field notes, October 1988).

19. Interview with YK, February 1990.

20. Observations of community group meetings that focused on the strip over a two-year period. Interview with merchant, November 1988.

21. Household interview 0–3.

22. In 1990, the sign incident was still being talked about. At the polls on Election Day, November 1990, upon seeing an Asian go in to vote, the local committeeman started talking about the signs again, as a group of established residents retold the story to one another seeking affirmation of their interpretations. Korean merchants bring up the topic frequently as well.

23. Household interview 0–5.

24. Weekly observations at four schools.

25. Participant observation in one sixth-grade classroom with 20 Latino students (14 in ESOL and 6 not) as well as 14 established students demonstrated that ESOL structured friendships.

26. If established residents did not know the specific nationality of an Asian, the label used was usually "Chinese," or in some cases Oriental. In Olney, "Korean" was often used as the generic Asian label. Spanish-speakers almost invariably referred to Asians as "chinos."

27. Household interviews 0–7, 0–8, 0–9.

28. Participation in the planning and execution of four activities (two festivals and two social actions) revealed this to be the common pattern.

29. At one event there had been no plans to label foods. As women set up the food table, they quickly prepared handwritten signs identifying their nationality and constructed boundaries to set their foods apart. In the second year of the event, they came prepared with flags and banners and arrived early to stake out prime space. The master of ceremonies at another event reported being pressured about the order of performances and their time allocations.

30. Most people have multiple national ancestries and see themselves as American in contrast to non-English speakers or white in contrast to their newcomer minority neighbors.

31. The Philadelphia Neighborhood Human Relations Projects were funded by a local foundation and administered by the Urban Coalition.

32. While several interested people in Port Richmond were willing to collaborate on a "March against Racism," communication was difficult because there were no organizations with office staff and message machines like those in Kensington. Often parish secretaries, who knew nothing about the activity, were the only points of contact and messages were delayed or went astray.

BIBLIOGRAPHY

Adams, Carolyn, David Bartelt, David Elesh, Ira Goldstein, Nancy Kleniewski, and William Yancey. *Philadelphia: Neighborhoods, Division and Conflict in a Post Industrial City*. Philadelphia: Temple University Press, 1991.

Bach, Robert. *The Changing Relations Project*. New York: Ford Foundation, 1993.

Binzen, Peter. *Whitetown, U.S.A.* New York: Random House, 1970.

Goldstein, Ira. "The Wrong Side of the Tracts: A Study of Residential Segregation in Philadelphia, 1930–1980." Unpublished doctoral dissertation. Philadelphia: Temple University, 1986.

Goode, Judith. "A Wary Welcome to the Neighborhood: Community Response to Immigrants." *Urban Anthropology* 19 (1990): 125–53.

Goode, Judith, and Juana McCormack. "Negotiating Hispanic Identity within a Multi-Ethnic Community." Paper delivered at the XV International Conference of the Latin American Studies Association, Miami, Florida, December 1990.

Goode, Judith, and Jo Anne Schneider. *Reshaping Ethnic and Racial Relations in Philadelphia: Immigrants in a Divided City*. Philadelphia: Temple University Press, 1994.

Goode, Judith, Jo Anne Schneider, and Sukey Blanc. "Transcending Boundaries and Closing Ranks: How Schools Shape Interrelations." In *Structuring Diversity*, L. Lamphere, ed. Chicago: University of Chicago Press, 1992.

Keefe, Susan E. "Introduction." In *Negotiating Ethnicity: The Impact of Anthropological Theory and Practice*, S. E. Keefe, ed. NAPA Bulletin no. 8. Washington, D.C.: American Anthropological Association, 1989, pp. 1–8.

Philadelphia Inquirer, Metropolitan Business Report, September 12, 1988.

Power, Edward. "Asian Immigrants Lend New Life to City's Sewing Industry." *Philadelphia Inquirer*, February 28, 1988.

Seder, Jean. *Voices of Kensington: Vanishing Mills, Vanishing Neighborhoods*. McLean, Va.: EPM Publications, 1990.

Stains, Lawrence, and John Marchese. "The Philly 200." *Philadelphia Magazine* 79 (April 1988): 145–70.

IV

The World Setting and Response

8

Ethnic Conflict at Home and Abroad: The United States in Comparative Perspective

James Kurth

The 1990s brought a renewed focus on ethnic conflict in the United States. The impact of immigration, the growth of the underclass, and the ascendancy of multiculturalism have together produced a sense that ethnic conflict will dominate American politics in the future. But the 1990s also have brought a renewed focus on ethnic conflict abroad. The impact of immigration in Western Europe, the collapse of communism, and the return of ethnic nationalism in Eastern Europe and in the former Soviet Union, and the "failed states" and ethnic massacres in Africa have together produced a sense that ethnic conflict will dominate international politics in the new era that has succeeded the era of the cold war.

This chapter will look at ethnic conflict in the United States from a comparative perspective, particularly in the light of the experiences of Western Europe and Eastern Europe. We will present three historical models of ethnic relations, demonstrating especially the relations of ethnic communities with the nation state—the Western European, the Eastern European, and the American. Within the American model, we will consider what we will call four motors of assimilation, and we will also consider these from a European perspective. We will conclude that Asian Americans are largely following a path that is best described by the traditional American model, that Mexican Americans are largely following a path that has much in common with the Eastern European model, and that African Americans are suspended, or rather split, between these two paths.

THE WESTERN EUROPEAN MODEL: THE CIVIC NATION

In Western Europe, the state existed before the nation, and it brought the nation into being over the course of several centuries. This meant that the state combined several prenational ethnic communities into one national society based upon some common denominator (usually a common language and literature) and some common dominator (usually a "modernizing monarchy"). These modernizing monarchies deemed it necessary and desirable to subordinate the distinct ethnic groups within their realms to a common culture.[1]

Where a degree of economic opportunity and social mobility existed, individuals might acquire this common culture of their own volition and on their way upward. The best example was Britain, particularly with the impetus of the Industrial Revolution. Where social mobility was more constrained, the state achieved the common culture through political and legal measures. State authority substituted for social mobility as the engine of cultural commonality. The best example was France, particularly with the inspiration of the Enlightenment.

The resulting conception of nationality was that the state creates the nation around a common culture, that the state and its laws define citizenship in the nation, and that the state may confer citizenship in the nation to particular persons who have become fully assimilated into the common culture.[2]

The Western European model—of the state creating the nation through composing a common culture—was adopted by certain states outside of Europe as they underwent their own modernization. This has been especially the case in East Asia (with Japan beginning in the late nineteenth century and with South Korea, Taiwan, and Singapore more recently). And, as we shall see below, it was even adopted by the United States from the 1910s through the 1930s, when the nation undertook a grand project known as "Americanization."

THE EASTERN EUROPEAN MODEL: THE ETHNIC NATION

The Western European conception of nationality is civic: defined by legal status with citizenship conferred by the state. In contrast, the Eastern European conception of nationality is ethnic: defined by genealogical history and with membership inherited at birth.[3]

In Eastern Europe, the nation existed before the state, and it brought the state into being largely in the course of one century, the nineteenth. Ethnic groups had already become nations but not yet states. This meant that the state was the creation of one newly-national ethnic community.

As in the East the nation that created the state was a particular ethnic community, the state was created in the image of that ethnic group. Any state would very well fit the particular community that created it (as Yugoslavia between the two world wars fit the Serbs, and Czechoslovakia fit the Czechs), but it would fit very imperfectly some other ethnic community that happened to be contained within the state (for example, the Croats and the Slovenes in Yugoslavia and the Slovaks and the Germans in Czechoslovakia).

The new Eastern European states tried to follow the Western European model with a program of cultural nationalization, but they had a far more difficult task than their Western counterparts. First, the different ethnic groups had already developed into nations more than had been the case in Western Europe earlier. In addition, economic opportunity and social mobility were even more constrained in Eastern Europe than in Western Europe. This drove some Eastern states to nationalizing methods that were even more ruthless and brutal than those in the West, for example, authoritarian repression and ethnic expulsions.

These Eastern conceptions of national identity did not just characterize the nineteenth and early twentieth centuries in the region, however. They are present there even today. Indeed, they reappeared with particular strength in the ruins of communism.

The basic problem in Eastern Europe has always been a Western concept that did not fit the Eastern reality well enough to turn the East into the West, but that did fit it well enough to tempt the East to create its own version of the West. The combination of Western ideology (rooted in the Enlightenment) and Eastern ethnicity (rooted in Orthodox Christianity) produced a distinctive Eastern kind of nationality.

The traditional non-national answer to this multinational condition of Eastern Europe has always been some version of a multinational empire. Before World War I, there were the Habsburg and the Ottoman empires; after World War II, the Soviet Union and Tito's Yugoslavia.

The Soviet and Yugoslav Communist parties served much the same function as the Habsburg and Ottoman dynasties, but being faced with nationalities that were now more organized and articulate than their ethnic predecessors, they, too, had to be more organized and more brutal than their dynastic predecessors. The Soviet Union and Yugoslavia were prison houses of nations, not just multinational empires. For many years, they managed to keep their subject peoples contained, to prevent both a jailbreak out of the prison or a prison riot among the inmates.

Eventually, however, all multinational empires fail, as they lose the interest and the will to impose order. At this point, there again reappears the ethnic-national answer to the multinational condition of Eastern Europe. This answer is what we have been hearing and seeing in Eastern Europe in the 1990s, most obviously in Bosnia and the rest of the former Yugoslavia.

The starkest possible illustration of this descent is given by *Schindler's List*. At one level, the film illustrates the crimes of Nazi Germany. At another level, however, it illustrates the failure of the Habsburg empire. All the scenes take place in what had been territories of Austria-Hungary (Cracow and Auschwitz had been in Austrian Galicia; Oskar Schindler's ''ammunition'' factory was in what had been Austrian Moravia). Schindler was originally from Moravia, the concentration camp commandant was originally from Vienna, and, of course, Hitler was originally from Austria. Anti-Semitism had been widespread in Central and Eastern Europe before World War I. It was especially intense and fevered, however, in the multinational cauldron of Austria-Hungary. The collapse of the Habsburg empire in 1918 released waves of ethnic conflict in general and of anti-Semitism in particular, which culminated a generation later in the Holocaust.

The Eastern European model—of one nation creating a state to impose a common culture on other nations—also has been adopted by certain states outside of Europe, as they have undergone their own modernization. This has been the case especially in the Middle East (for example, Iraq, Syria, and Turkey). In this region, however, the state has been even more artificial and the ethnic communities have been even more tribal than in Eastern Europe.

THE AMERICAN MODEL: THE ASSIMILATED NATION

Whereas in Western Europe the state existed before the nation, and in Eastern Europe the nation existed before the state, in America the individual has been seen as existing before both. Of course, the original colonies in the seventeenth century were actually founded by persons who arrived in America as an organized group (most famously, the Pilgrims with their Mayflower Compact). Later generations of immigrants, however, usually arrived as individuals or as nuclear families. The idea that the individual existed before the state and nation has put distinct limits on both these entities as the definers of American identity.

In some senses, there was already an American nation or people (really an Anglo-American people) at the time of the creation of the American state (actually the federal republic established by the Constitution in 1789). As we have seen, in Eastern Europe, the nation also existed before the state, and there it created the state in its own image. This was also the case in America, where the Anglo-Americans created the United States in the image of more than a century of English political theories and practices.[4] However, the content of that state, being Anglo-American or even English, had far more in common with Western Europe than with Eastern Europe. In particular, the definition of nationality was civic rather than ethnic, legal rather than genealogical, individual rather than communal.

In America, then, the process of creating the state bears more similarities to that in Eastern Europe, but the product of the created state bears more similarities to that in Western Europe. This combination of Western and Eastern elements has been one factor making for a distinctive American definition of nationality and lends credibility to the idea of American exceptionalism.

Much more central to American exceptionalism, however, is the idea that the individual is prior to both the state and the nation. This idea is grounded in many American realities, but probably the most fundamental is the process of immigration and assimilation, the great drama in which individuals have been drawn out of their ethnic communities and assimilated into American society. This process can be seen as having four dynamics or dimensions. We shall call these the four motors of assimilation.

Four Motors of Assimilation

The Ideological Motor

Many interpreters of American nationality have argued that American identity is defined by the acceptance of particular ideals. These ideals are centered upon the freedom of the individual and are articulated in the "American creed."[5] In this conception, America is a "nation of immigrants," who as individuals left their old ethnic communities and identities and became Americans by adhering to the American creed. As long as people living in the United States see themselves as individuals and as believers in the American creed, there will be a strong and cohesive American identity and nationality.

The Economic Motor

Other interpreters of American nationality have put prime emphasis on the high degree of economic opportunity and social mobility in the United States. This has given immigrants the incentive to "get up and go," to achieve individual advancement even at the expense of communal obligations, and to think of themselves as individuals. These economically advancing, socially mobile individuals naturally have then adopted the American creed of liberal individualism. As long as people living in the United States have economic opportunity and social mobility, there will be a strong and cohesive American identity and nationality.

The Linguistic Motor

Some social analysts believe that a central element, even necessary condition, of American nationality has been linguistic uniformity around the common English language. In the past, this has been brought about partly by political means, such as language laws and public education. The principal factor, however, has been the economic motor, which requires English facility as a condition for upward mobility. As long as people living within the United States speak a common English language, there will be a strong and cohesive American nationality, or at least the necessary foundation for it.

The Intermarriage Motor

Finally, some social analysts hold that full completion of the process of immigration and assimilation is found in intermarriage. At the core of communal identity is the strong extended family; at the core of American identity is the strong, freely choosing, individual. The extended family is weakened by the freedom of individual choice, most fundamentally in the choice of a marriage partner. As long as ethnic differences are dissolving and disappearing within the crucible of intermarriage, there will be the basis for a strong and cohesive American nationality.

It is natural enough for Americans to think that the main motor of assimilation has been the ideological one. This comports most nicely with Americans' conception of themselves as strong individuals who freely choose to be Americans because of lofty ideals.

Europeans have a somewhat different perspective, however. They have seen the failure of numerous ideological projects (including that of liberalism) over the two centuries since the American Revolution (and since the French Revolution). By itself, an ideological motor is not going to go very far, or at least last very long. Europeans are inclined instead to credit the success of assimilation in America to some additional factors.

One of these is the economic motor. Europeans have long seen the greater economic opportunity and social mobility in the United States to be the most important contrast between Europe and America. Another factor, however, is one where Europeans have seen an important similarity between Europe and America, at least for the first half of the twentieth century. This factor is the power of the state, which lies at the base of the ideological motor. As it turns out, the actual development of the American creed, the construction of the ideological motor, bears some similarities with the Western Europe model.

THE AMERICANIZATION PROJECT

The current era of high immigration into the United States is not the first time that this country has experienced large numbers of immigrants from different cultures, with prospects for their acceptance of the dominant culture seemingly problematic. A similar condition existed a century ago, particularly from the 1880s to the 1920s, when the culture formed within the United States by Western Europeans (principally by those of British descent) had to confront large numbers of immigrants from Eastern and Southern Europe (principally Poles, Jews, and Italians). It then appeared that the United States was becoming what is now called a "multicultural society."[6]

The reaction of the political and intellectual elites of that time to their multicultural reality was precisely the opposite of that of the political and intellectual elites of today. They did not rejoice in multicultural society and dedicate themselves to making it even more multicultural. Rather, they undertook a massive and systematic program of Americanization, imposing on the new immigrants and on their children the English language, Anglo-American history, and American civics (what Robert Bellah would later term the American "civil religion" and what many would term the "American creed"). The Anglo-American elite was aided in its grand project of Americanization by the booming U.S.

economy during this period, which gave immigrants ample economic reasons to assimilate, and by the restrictive immigration law of 1924, which essentially halted immigration from Eastern and Southern Europe and allowed the Americanization process to operate upon and shape a settled mass.

This grand project of Americanization was relentless and even ruthless. Many persons were oppressed and victimized by it, and many rich and meaningful cultural islands were swept away. But the achievements of that project were awesome, as well as awful. In particular, when the United States entered into its greatest struggles of the twentieth century, first World War II and then the cold war, it did so as a national state, rather than as a multicultural society. (Hitler consistently underestimated the United States because he thought it was the latter rather than the former; his understanding of American society dated from the time of World War I.) It was because of the Americanization project that the United States could become the leader and the defender of Western Europe and of Western values throughout the world.

THE CULMINATION OF INDIVIDUALISM AMONG EUROPEAN AMERICANS

The Americanization project faded away in the 1950s, having achieved its objectives. For a time, it was replaced with the ideal of a pluralist society. The reality, however, was the relentless workings of the four motors of assimilation, which were completing the transformation of European Americans into an individualist society.

Europeans have also long been sensitive to the negative consequences of individualism. The greatest European interpreter of America, Alexis de Tocqueville, acutely analyzed the virtues of individualism in the United States, but also its vices.[7] Later European social analysts have tended to emphasize even more the negative aspects.

The individualist dynamic by itself can lead to social pathologies, particularly personal emptiness or criminal behavior. These have become so evident in the past two or three decades that some American social analysts, including Nathan Glazer, who presents his views in Chapter 9 of this volume, have joined European ones in arguing for the need to preserve communities. Most American social analysts, however, still seem more fearful of the potential consequences of the communal dynamic, particularly political stalemate or ethnic conflict ("Balkanization").

The best mix might appear to be a dynamic tension between the two tendencies, the individual and the communal. For a long time, this was largely the case with all the ethnic groups that immigrated from Europe, with, however, the communal tendency weakening and the individual tendency strengthening over time.

In the last two decades or so, the individual tendency among Americans of European origin has become very pronounced. In part, this is the result of the four motors of assimilation, especially the fulfillment of social mobility. In part, as Gary Rubin argues in Chapter 2 of this volume, it is the result of the legal decisions of the Supreme Court (the use of the Fourteenth Amendment to enforce the First Amendment to free individual expression from community constraints), along with the "expressive individualism" of the generation of the 1960s.[8] In any event, the consequence is that by the mid-1990s communal or ethnic identity among white Americans has become extremely weak, and among the young it is only vestigial.

In the 1990s, then, the four motors of assimilation have largely completed the process of transforming the different ethnic communities of European Americans into a national society of assimilated, even interchangeable, Americans. A nation of immigrants has been turned into a nation of individuals.

The ethnic issues of the 1990s, however, do not involve relations among Americans whose origins lie in Europe. They involve relations among these Americans and those whose origins lie in the continents beyond Europe, that is, Asia, Latin America, and Africa. We will now turn to the three great communities of Asian Americans, Latino Americans, and African Americans. For some within these communities, the American model and its four motors of assimilation are still working. But for others, the model and its motors have clearly broken down.

Three Communities and Their Different Paths

Asian Americans

The path that Asian Americans will take is still a matter of debate. Some emphasize the racial differences between Asian Americans and European Americans and argue that Asian Americans will always be victims of racial discrimination. Others emphasize the educational achievements of Asian Americans and argue that assimilation is progressing rapidly.[9]

By now, there is a good deal of evidence pointing to the latter path, that of assimilation in the traditional American way. Although Asian Americans are "strangers from a different shore,"[10] they are like Europeans in having voluntarily crossed a large ocean to get to America. Among most Asian-American communities, assimilation is following the pattern of earlier European groups. This is especially the case with those Asian Americans with a cultural tradition that values formal learning (for example, the Confucian examination system—Chinese, Japanese, Koreans, and Vietnamese—or the British-colonial educational legacy—Indians and Pakistanis). Other Asian-American communities appear to be assimilating, but at a slower rate (for example, Filipinos). The greatest difficulties are experienced by those who have arrived in America with experience only in subsistence agriculture (for example, the Hmong of Laos).

Latino Americans

The Latino-American community comprises principally Mexican Americans, Puerto Ricans, and Cuban Americans. Mexican Americans form more than 65 percent of the Latino-American population. They are also likely to take a different path from Asian Americans or even from Puerto Ricans and Cuban Americans.

From a European perspective, the Mexican-American presence in the United States is an old and familiar story. A country is defeated in war, part of it is annexed by the victorious power, and its population is subordinated to the level of second-class citizens or worse. History moves on, however, and conditions change. Eventually the balance of power, or at least the balance of population, between the dominant people and the subordinate people shifts, to the advantage of the latter.[11] There were several such cases in Eastern Europe during the last few decades before World War I (for example, the Poles in the eastern part of Germany and the Czechs and the South Slavs in Austria-Hungary).

From this European perspective, it becomes important that the rate of Mexican immigration into the United States exceeds the rate of Mexican-American assimilation into a common culture and that Mexican Americans are retaining the Spanish language for use in almost all activities, including politics. Similar processes happened with many nationalities within Eastern Europe during the past century.

There is now a new Mexican nation growing up on the land stretching from Texas to California, on the territory of the old American nation (and on the former territory of the even older Mexican nation, before the Texan Revolution of 1836 and the Mexican War of 1846–1848). In some senses, this new nation is a blend of American and Mexican features, a sort of "Amerexico."[12] In other senses, its features are overwhelmingly Mexican, a sort of "New Mexico," that is much greater in territorial extent than the literal State of New Mexico.

The construction of Amerexico is facilitated by most contemporary liberals who encourage Mexican Americans to think of themselves as a minority and as victims, rather than as immigrants on the way to assimilation. It is facilitated also by most businesses in the Southwest, especially agricultural ones, who have long sought large numbers of low-wage, low-skilled laborers.

Amerexico is a society whose upper or capital-owning class is American, whose professional and middle classes are largely American but partly Mexican American, and whose working and lower classes are Mexican American. It is characterized by a racial division of labor, a correlation between class and color. As such, it bears similarities to the societies of Eastern Europe as they existed up to World War II, which were also characterized by an ethnic division of labor.

Cuban Americans, in contrast, appear to be on the path of assimilation in the traditional American way. This is especially the case with those Cuban Americans who are largely of European (Spanish), rather than African, origin. These are also largely professional or middle class in their social origins from pre-Castro Cuba. Their story has more in common with European Americans and even with most Asian Americans, than it does with that of most Mexican Americans.[13]

Puerto Ricans, in contrast again, appear to be on neither the traditional path of assimilation nor the path of a new nation on the territory of the continental United States. Most Puerto Rican immigrants to the mainland are of African as well as Spanish origin. Their path in the future will likely be very similar to that of African Americans.[14]

African Americans

Although the Mexican-American presence in the United States has clear analogues in the history of Eastern Europe, this is not the case with the African-American presence. In some senses, the African-American experience can be interpreted through the conventional American prism. Although the way that Africans arrived in America from the seventeenth century to the nineteenth century was involuntary rather than voluntary, "transportation" rather than immigration, the way that African Americans arrived in the northern and western United States in the half-century from the 1910s to the 1960s was voluntary, and this "great migration"[15] has much in common with traditional immigration. In the view of some liberals, the assimilationist trajectory of African Americans really began only in the first half of the twentieth century, and it was given full political and legal recognition only with the civil rights achievements of the 1960s. If that is so, African Americans are on the same path and progressing at roughly the same rate as earlier immigrants from Europe, particularly those whose previous experience was largely in agricultural labor (for example, the Irish and the Poles).

In other senses, however, the African-American experience can be interpreted as having some similarities with the Mexican-American experience. There is evidence of a growing separation between about half of the African-American population, especially that part called the "underclass," and most of the other American population.[16]

The underclass in American cities forms an unassimilated, unassimilating, and probably unassimilatable people, which is scattered across the American landscape in a series of urban enclaves or islands. Together, these underclass islands form a sort of "African-American Archipelago."

The African-American Archipelago is a society whose upper or capital-owning class consists largely of absentee landlords who are white Americans, whose small professional and middle classes are largely American but partly African American, and whose lower class and underclass are African American. There is also a Puerto Rican version of this society.[17] Given the pervasive unemployment within it, it is not quite accurate to say that this society is characterized by a racial division of labor, but it is certainly characterized by a correlation between class and color. As such, it bears similarities with some of the islands in another archipelago, the West Indies.

It is clear that, with regard to many Mexican Americans, African Americans, and Puerto Ricans, the traditional American model of assimilation is not working. One of the root causes of the breakdown of the model has been a double transformation that has occurred in the economic context of ethnic relations in the past two decades.

The Double Economic Transformation

The 1990s have seen the maturing of two economic developments that have had major consequences for national assimilation versus ethnic conflict: first, there has been the transformation of the most advanced countries, especially the United States, from industrial to postindustrial economies; second, there has been the transformation of the international economy into a truly global economy.

The Transformation from Industrial to Postindustrial Economy

At the most obvious level, this means the replacement of industrial production with service processes. These changes have been noted and discussed for more than a generation, at least since Daniel Bell published his seminal *The Coming of Post-Industrial Society* (1973). But their maturity has come only in the past decade, as Peter Drucker has recently discussed.[18]

The Transformation of the International Economy into a Global One

At the most obvious level, this means the replacement of national production that is engaged in international trade with global production that is engaged in a worldwide market in trade, investment, and technology. These changes, too, have been noted and discussed for a generation, ever since Raymond Vernon published his seminal *Sovereignty at Bay* (1971). But their maturity also has come only in the past decade, as Vernon has recently discussed in his *Defense and Dependence in the Global Economy* (1992).[19]

The globalization of production means the relocation of industrial production from high-wage and high-skill advanced-industrial countries to low-wage but high-skill newly industrial countries (NICs). This is the de-industrialization of the advanced countries, the dark half of the postindustrial transformation. The two transformations—from industrial to postindustrial and from international to global—are intimately connected.

This double economic transformation has caused a stalling of the economic motor of assimilation for those ethnic and racial groups that, by the early 1970s, had largely assimilated only up to the level of industrial labor and not yet to the level of technical (postindustrial) labor. This was especially the case with African Americans. Moreover, most Mexican Americans and Puerto Ricans had not even reached the level of skilled industrial labor.

The Stalling of the Four Motors

More generally, there has been a stalling of each of the four motors of assimilation in the past decade or two.

The Ideological Motor

Most liberals have replaced the ideal of individualism with that of multiculturalism. Much of the American political and intellectual class now thinks of America as a multicultural society. Their preferred cultures are those of African Americans, Latino Americans, and some Asian Americans. These liberals demonstrate contempt for the cultures of Europe (''dead white European males'') and even for the American creed.

The Economic Motor

This motor of assimilation—moving immigrants up the class ladder on the successive rungs of peasant labor, unskilled industrial labor, skilled industrial labor, and then the lower middle class or even the professional class—operated effectively and efficiently in an industrial economy with plenty of blue-collar jobs. It operates much less well in a postindustrial, high-technology, global economy with a rapidly shrinking number of blue-collar jobs. A large percentage of African Americans and Mexican Americans confront an economy that no longer has the rungs for skilled industrial labor, and they thus remain stuck as unskilled labor or even in an underclass.

The Linguistic Motor

Educational authorities now encourage the continuation of Spanish and the development of Black English as the basis for separate linguistic communities. They are reinforced and confirmed by multiculturalists, who hold the ideal of a common language in contempt and who exalt the ideal of a bilingual or multilingual society.

The Intermarriage Motor

Given the weakening of the first three dynamics, the dynamic of intermarriage is weak also. It seems to be the case that there is little intermarriage between lower-class African Americans or Mexican Americans and other Americans.

In summary, the last two decades have seen a stalling of the four motors of assimilation for African Americans and Mexican Americans at the lower levels of the class structure. This stalling has resulted from transformations that are so deep that they are unlikely to be reversed. The prospects, then, are for America to cease to be one nation and to become three nations—assimilated America, African America, and Mexican America, all inhabiting the territory of the not-so-United States.

A DIFFERENT KIND OF AMERICAN
EXCEPTIONALISM

In one sense, this might be seen as the end of the American model of ethnic relations—and the end of a central pillar of American exceptionalism. In respect to its European-American (and also Asian-American) populations, America has acted in a typically American (and generally un-European) way by fully assimilating them into Americans. In respect to its African-American and Mexican-American populations, however, America appears to be ending up in a European, even Eastern European, condition.

In another sense, however, this condition of three peoples on American territory has always been the American condition. More than 160 years ago, that great European observer of democracy in America, Alexis de Tocqueville, wrote about "the three races in the United States" (he referred to them as whites, blacks, and Indians), and he observed that the relations among them was one of the features that made America exceptional.[20] The racial relations in America, like democracy in America, were unique, but these racial relations also represented a fateful, and perhaps fatal, contradiction to that democracy. Racial relations were the distinctive feature of America even before democracy. American democracy may be said to have begun with the election of Thomas Jefferson as president in 1800; American racial relations may be said to have begun with the first importation of blacks into Virginia in 1619.

Can there be a distinctively American solution to this distinctively American problem of racial relations? It seems unlikely. The distinctive American solution to the problem of ethnic relations in the past was assimilation of individuals. The stalling of the four motors of assimilation means that this past solution is no longer working for African Americans and Mexican Americans, for blacks and browns.

We can also be confident that there will not be a Western European solution to this problem. Assimilation into a common culture imposed by state authority was possible only in the America of the first half of the twentieth century and then only with ample support from a growing industrial economy and its attendant social mobility. Instead, the American political and intellectual class of our time prefers either to impose multiculturalism by state authority or to impose nothing at all. For a Western European solution, then, it is too late.

We can also hope that there will not be an Eastern European "solution" to this problem, that is, growing ethnic separation that culminates in episodes of authoritarian repression and ethnic expulsion. For an Eastern European solution, it should always be too early.

Some problems are never solved. They turn out to be not so much problems that have solutions, but rather conditions that one must live with as best one can, sometimes for years, sometimes for generations. Each generation of Americans has had to live with some version of the American racial condition. It is likely that, for as long as there is an America, each generation of Americans in the future will have to do so also.

America was born with the tragic flaw, the original sin, of the enslavement of Africans. It grew to maturity with the conquest of Mexicans. It will have to live with the consequences of these acts for the rest of its life. The real question is not how to solve the problem. It is how to live with the condition with patience, decency, and wisdom.

NOTES

1. James Kurth, "The Post-Modern State," *The National Interest* 28 (Summer 1992): 26–29.

2. Liah Greenfeld, *Nationalism: Five Paths to Modernity* (Cambridge, Mass.: Harvard University Press, 1992), introduction and chapters 1–2.

3. Ibid.; William Pfaff, *The Wrath of Nations: Civilization and the Fury of Nationalism* (New York: Simon and Schuster, 1993); also James Kurth, "Eastern Question, Western Answer," *The National Interest* 34 (Winter 1993/94): 96–97.

4. Bernard Bailyn, *The Ideological Origins of the American Revolution* (Cambridge, Mass: Harvard University Press, 1967).

5. Arthur Schlesinger, Jr., *The Disuniting of America: Reflections on a Multicultural Society* (New York: W. W. Norton and Company, 1992).

6. James Kurth, "The *Real* Clash," *The National Interest* 37 (Fall 1994): 12–13.

7. Alexis de Tocqueville, *Democracy in America*, trans. by Henry Reeve as rev. by Frances Bowen and ed. by Phillip Bradley (New York: Knopf, 1945).

8. On expressive individualism, see Lawrence M. Friedman, *The Republic of Choice: Law, Authority and Culture* (Cambridge, Mass.: Harvard University Press, 1990).

9. Nathan Caplan, John K. Whitmore, and Marcella H. Choy, *The Boat People and Achievement in America: A Study of Family Life, Hard Work and Cultural Values* (Ann Arbor: University of Michigan Press, 1989).

10. Ronald T. Takaki, *Strangers from A Different Shore: A History of Asian Americans* (New York: Penguin Books, 1990).

11. Rodolfo Acuma, *Occupied America: A History of Chicanos*, 3d ed. (New York: Harper & Row, 1988).

12. Peter Andreas, "The Making of Amerexico: (Mis)Handling Illegal Immigration," *World Policy Journal* (Summer 1994): 45–56.

13. On Cuban Americans, see Joe R. Feagin and Clairece Booker Feagin, *Racial and Ethnic Relations*, 4th ed. (Englewood Cliffs, N.J.: Prentice Hall, 1993), Chap. 10.

14. On Puerto Ricans, see ibid.; also Thomas Sowell, *Ethnic America: A History* (New York: Basic Books, 1981).

15. Nicholas Lemann, *The Promised Land: The Great Black Migration and How It Changed America* (New York: Knopf, 1991).

16. Andrew Hacker, *Two Nations: Black and White, Separate, Hostile, Unequal* (New York: Ballantine Books, 1992); Elijah Anderson, "The Code of the Streets," *The Atlantic Monthly* (May 1994): 81–94; also his *Streetwise: Race, Class and Change in an Urban Community* (Chicago: University of Chicago Press, 1990).

17. Nicholas Lemann, "The Other Underclass," *The Atlantic Monthly* (December 1991): 96–110.

18. Daniel Bell, *The Coming of Post-Industrial Society: A Venture in Social Forecasting* (New York: Basic Books, 1973); Peter F. Drucker, "The Age of Social Transformation," *The Atlantic Monthly* (November 1994): 53–80.

19. Raymond Vernon, *Sovereignty at Bay: The Multinational Spread of U.S. Enterprises* (New York: Basic Books, 1971); Raymond Vernon and Ethan B. Kapstein, eds., *Defense and Dependence in the Global Economy* (Washington, D.C.: Congressional Quarterly, 1992).

20. de Tocqueville, *Democracy in America*, vol. 1, chap. 18, "The Three Races in the United States."

BIBLIOGRAPHY

Acuna, Rodolfo. *Occupied America: A History of Chicanos*. 3rd ed. New York: Harper & Row, 1988.

Anderson, Elijah. *Streetwise: Race, Class and Change in an Urban Community*. Chicago: University of Chicago Press, 1990.

Andreas, Peter. "The Making of Amerexico: (Mis)Handling Illegal Immigration." *World Policy Journal* (Summer 1994).

Caplan, Nathan, John K. Whitmore, and Marcella H. Choy. *The Boat People and Achievement in America: A Study of Family Life, Hard Work and Cultural Values*. Ann Arbor: University of Michigan Press, 1989.

Feagin, Joe R., and Clairece Booker Feagin. *Racial and Ethnic Relations*. 4th ed. Englewood Cliffs, N.J.: Prentice Hall, 1993.

Greenfield, Liah. *Nationalism: Five Paths to Modernity*. Cambridge, Mass.: Harvard University Press, 1992.

Hacker, Andrew. *Two Nations: Black and White, Separate, Hostile, Unequal.* New York: Ballantine Books, 1992.

Lemann, Nicholas. *The Promised Land: The Great Black Migration and How It Changed America.* New York: Knopf, 1991.

Schlesinger, Arthur, Jr. *The Disuniting of America: Reflections on a Multicultural Society.* New York: W. W. Norton and Company, 1992.

Sowell, Thomas. *Ethnic America: A History.* New York: Basic Books. 1981.

Takaki, Ronald T. *Strangers from a Different Shore: A History of Asian Americans.* New York: Penguin Books, 1990.

de Tocqueville, Alexis. *Democracy in America.* Trans. by Henry Reeve, as rev. by Frances Bowen and ed. by Phillip Bradley. New York: Knopf, 1945.

9

How Should We Talk about Intergroup Conflict?

Nathan Glazer

A long time ago, before the civil rights revolution, when sociologists and anthropologists studied race relations in the South, they sometimes used the term "the etiquette of race relations" to refer to the expected behavior of blacks towards whites, and whites toward blacks. It was a rather odd term—drawn, as it was, from the practices of formal social intercourse and reminding us of tea parties and appropriate greetings—to use for a system of relations in which the transgression of the appropriate forms sometimes meant lynching and death. There are many descriptions of this etiquette that prevailed in the days when the relations between whites and blacks in the South were strictly governed by the assumption of white superiority in all respects: for example, "the Negro, when addressing a white person, is expected to use a title such as 'Sah,' 'Mistah,' 'Boss,' etc., while the white must never use such titles of respect to the Negro but should address him by his first name or as 'Boy.' "[1]

Fortunately, that is all now history. But I am reminded of this notion of an etiquette of race relations because of a number of serious conflicts that have emerged in recent years in intergroup relations, conflicts that raise directly the questions of how we speak and how we should speak, about painful and divisive issues.

I have in mind, for example, the arguments that have raged over the speeches of Louis Farrakhan and Khalid Muhammed on the campuses of Howard University and other universities, and, even more, the arguments over what is the appropriate response to such speeches—by Jews, by black leaders, by black students, by others. Should the Anti-Defamation League have taken a full-page advertisement to reprint Khalid Muhammed's speech, as it did? Should black leaders have immediately denounced it? Should Jewish leaders have called on black leaders to denounce it? Should students at Howard University have said that they found some good in the speech? Should they have been denounced for saying so? And so on. I have in mind, too, all the issues that have come up on college campuses regarding what is called "hate speech" and the conflicts over campus codes of behavior that have been proposed and adopted to deal with racial epithets—or what are conceived to be epithets by one individual or group of individuals, but may be considered high jinks or legitimate reference to race and difference by another. Yet another and particularly difficult group of issues is raised by faculty who write and talk about group differences and group power. These issues are epitomized by the cases of Professors Michael Levin and Leonard Jeffries at the City College of New York and of Professor Tony Martin of Wellesley College.[2]

More recently we have had the issue of the scholarly discussion of race differences initiated by the publication of *The Bell Curve* by the late Professor Richard Herrnstein of Harvard and the controversial social policy analyst Charles Murray.[3] The book deals with the significance for all sorts of behavior and social problems of differences in individual intelligence. For most of its length, the issue of race is not addressed, but there is an important chapter on race. Individual differences in intelligence and various other test scores seems to be a safe enough topic—we all take the existence of such differences for granted; however, one can make averages and medians for a collection of individuals, and, if these are defined by race, the issue becomes explosive. So it was with *The Bell Curve*.

The issue of "etiquette," of how we talk about these matters, arises to begin with because of an initial utterance or an initial piece of writing. The specific content of what is said or written, the audience to which it is addressed, the tone that accompanies it—all raise questions of an appropriate etiquette. But there is also an appropriate etiquette of response, by various interested parties, and how these responses should be responded to—and so on, in an infinite regress it seems of rancor and discord. In contrast to the forms of social life, for which we have various arbiters, such as Emily Post for the more formal past, and Judith Martin for the looser and more disorderly present, we have not agreed on etiquette of proper speech and response in the area of race relations. Or, rather, we have had an established, informal code. Under this code, which prevailed, let us say, from roughly the 1950s until recent years, any reference to group difference could only be to favorable differences (even though, logically, to refer favorably to one group meant to refer unfavorably, even if only by implication, to others).

Two problems have developed with this code, a code that was created and existed in the name of good race relations: First, it is increasingly transgressed, as we see in some of the cases I have mentioned, and once it is widely transgressed, complex issues of response develop, as was demonstrated in the controversy over the invitation to Louis Farrakhan to participate in the black summit. Second, the informal code tended to favor the suppression of discourse, assertion, and argument on issues that the general public or some part of it felt was important but that the informal code of the etiquette of racial discourse asserted was not appropriate for public discussion. The problem with the informal code of the etiquette of good race or intergroup relations may be summed up as follows: On the one hand, there are the prohibited subjects; on the other hand, there is the question of truth, which may be uncomfortable for one group or another—for example, differences in intelligence, differences in rates of apprehension for criminal acts, and the high representation of Jews in the media. On the intelligence question or the issue of the Jewish role in the media, perhaps the code still prevails—just barely. On the crime issue, it has quite broken down.

One possible approach to dealing with this problem of the proper etiquette of discourse on race relations is not easily available to us in the United States: that is, fixing in law a standard as to what can be said and not be said in regard to group differences, with criminal or civil consequences if the rules are broken. This is not an easy solution, for it is no simple matter to formulate such a set of rules; but once they become law—and in some nations they have—they serve to put a floor to some degree on what can be said and advocated. Since 1965, England has had a Race Relations Act, which prohibits words or publications ''likely to stir up hatred . . . on grounds of color, race, or ethnic or national origins,'' and there have been prosecutions under it. Apparently, it is present in the consciousness of writers: P. D. James, in a recent interview I saw on public television, refers to it as one constraint on what mystery story writers can write. There is an International Covenant on Civil and

Political Rights and an International Convention on the Elimination of All Forms of Racial Discrimination, and France, India, Brazil, Argentina, and perhaps other countries have passed legislation pursuant to these international human rights declarations against hate speech.[4] Canada has a national statute, as have Australia and New Zealand.[5] There have been prosecutions for Holocaust denial in Canada and in France.

The reason this approach is not available to us in the United States is the First Amendment to the Constitution. From that simple proscription, "Congress shall make no law . . . abridging the freedom of speech, or of the press," there has flowed a body of law that I am sure would astonish the framers and adopters of that Amendment. Consequently, it is taken for granted by most commentators that to set the terms of legitimate discourse by national, state, or local legislation by formulating some common code, some agreed on limits and principles, is simply not possible here. Perhaps if it were possible to have such legislation here, it might serve to introduce a greater level of reason and civility in discussion of intergroup issues; perhaps it would not. It would be of value to study the experience of Canada, England, France, and other countries in which there has been legal action under their laws to restrict racist speech or publication.

Some legal commentators have argued that our First Amendment does not pose a necessary bar to such legislation, but they are in the minority within the legal community, and we have no examples of any governmental body trying to produce such a code in the United States. The First Amendment, as interpreted by the Supreme Court, is commonly believed to prohibit such limitations on speech, whether in the form of group libel laws or of laws forbidding speech that might provoke group disharmony and public disorder. Under our Constitution and our laws, we are more likely to see a racist demonstration protected by the police than banned.

The prohibition of the First Amendment now extends far beyond public legislatures. Colleges and universities trying to establish speech codes have run up against the First Amendment because these codes can be challenged in court and have been challenged successfully. Nor is it only public colleges that are affected. Private colleges, too, are now so intertwined, in their financing and regulations, with public authorities that it is very unlikely they have any power to limit speech in the interest of group harmony greater than that of public colleges. In the past, the presidents of Harvard and Yale, institutions that epitomize the American private university, have both said that the First Amendment would limit what they considered to be acceptable in a campus code of behavior and that no code could ban behavior that would be acceptable under the First Amendment, as interpreted by the courts.

This is not to suggest that in the absence of the First Amendment it would be easy to establish such codes, whether for communities or campuses. But the First Amendment makes the legal problem relatively easy: Hardly anything would pass muster as being so offensive, so outrageous, so likely to provoke riot and disorder as to be susceptible to legal limit, control, and prohibition. That still leaves open the question of what, in the absence of formal codes and powers limiting speech, should be our principles?

The term ''etiquette'' reminds us that we don't necessarily have to handle these matters through laws and codes. Ideally, we can handle them through a commonly accepted set of standards; and these standards can be maintained, as etiquette is, by the commonly accepted view of what just isn't done. The sanctions for transgression become expressions of disapproval, rather than formal proceedings leading to punishment, and these do work in well-ordered settings.

Thus, a few years ago, at Harvard, one student placed a Confederate flag outside her window. The college newspaper and many officials and students indicated their disapproval. Another student in protest hung a swastika outside *her* window. Various student groups met and talked, and the matter ended with both flags removed. The university took no formal action to remove either flag. Had the issue been covered by a code, with formal procedures for sanction and punishment, I think matters overall would have been worse. The first student, who was ideologically committed to the right to publicly celebrate her southern background, would probably have gone to court, various alumni would have been found to support her, and the matter would have ended up on the editorial pages of the *Wall Street Journal*. I am not suggesting that what happened was an ideal solution, that everyone was satisfied, or that there was not a residue of resentment, anger, and hurt feelings, only that even in the absence of a code, or when a code does not apply, there exists a host of informal controls, which may or may not be effective.

I am no friend of the argument that we must expand by judicial interpretation of our constitutional protections the legal remedies of those offended by speech or publication. I am suspicious of the effort to make illegal some kinds of speech—or ''words that wound,'' as in the title of the book in which Mari Matsuda, Richard Delgado, Charles Lawrence, and Kimberle Crenshaw argue for such. ''Words that wound'' can, indeed, be epithets, "assaultive speech," about which no reasonable persons can disagree, words that are personally hurtful and harmful and that should play no role in public or private life. However, the issue of whether there should be available a legal response, criminal or civil, to my mind raises primarily practical questions, not questions of principle that defend the right of someone to be offensive and hurtful to another person.

The problem is that words that wound to one party may be words of truth to another. Can we make a distinction on the basis of motive: These words have the appearance of truth but are really meant to wound; those words have the appearance of words expressed in anger or hate, but are trying to reach, and to spread, the truth? Consider advertisements that challenge the truth of the Holocaust: they are presented with all the accoutrements of truth-seeking and scholarship; yet the objectives to which they are addressed are so outlandish and outrageous that the sober, scholarly appearance is a simple lie when it comes to uncovering the motive. I feel quite confident of my capacity to distinguish motives when it comes to Holocaust denial. But I am also aware, speaking of my own motives, that arguments I have made, in the past, against some strong forms of affirmative action, on grounds of principle, on grounds of effectiveness, on grounds of consequences, have been taken by others to be motivated by self- or group-interest, or by racial antagonism.

Yet another distinction we can make among "words that wound" is between words that are intended to advance good group relations and words that are intended to increase group disharmony. This is also a matter of motive, but here the difference is not between the intention to wound others as against the intention to advance the truth, but between the intention to harm group relations versus the intention to advance understanding. Consider the argument about Jews and slavery. Undoubtedly, Jewish colonial merchants were involved in the slave trade. Undoubtedly, some Jews were slaveholders. Most people think these are matters of such small consequence that to raise them today, regardless of their truth content, can only mean that the motive is to increase black antagonism to Jews. I think so, too. And yet, as opposed to Holocaust denial, there is a kernel of truth content in the Jews-and-slavery assertions. Jewish merchants, like other merchants at the time, were involved in the slave trade.

But now, suppose the truth content and its significance rise. The power of the assertion to wound or to worsen race relations still exists. In contrast to the issue of Jews and slavery, in which a minimal involvement two hundred or more years ago is blown out of proportion, there are other instances involving issues that are alive in the present and of urgent significance. Consider differences in intelligence among groups, for example, which must have bearing on questions concerning possible discrimination against black students or faculty or simply a fair selection among those with similar qualifications; or the issue of the role of blacks in crime, where a similar question arises as to whether we deal with discrimination that results in these great group disparities in arrests and imprisonment or whether we deal with real differences. Underlying these two issues, troubling as they are, is the even more troubling issue, as to whether the disparities can be explained by differences in social environment, in which case one can at least imagine public and social interventions, or by some genetic base. Here one must report that in more and more fields biological explanations of behavior are receiving solid scientific support. Science is coming to the support of the most painful explanations of group differences.

Consider another issue, troubling in quite a different way: the assertion that Jews control the press. This is quite different in its impact on Jews from an assertion that blacks are intellectually inferior. In both cases, we would agree there are questions of evidence, argument, and scientific research—in the grandest sense questions of truth—even though, in these as in so many important questions, one can only approach truth and correct error, but rarely get to *the* truth. One can conduct studies, as many have, of differences in average achievement on IQ and other tests, consider the validity of these tests, consider the various factors that might lead to group differential performance, and the like. The scientific literature on this is large, though it is evaluated differently by different investigators. But the mere raising of the question, however cautiously, however bounded by qualifications, is wounding to individual blacks. One can well understand that the impact of raising such a question is significant in creating self-doubt and reminding individuals of times, not long distant, when blacks were excluded from many educational opportunities.

The impact of the charge that Jews control the press is quite different when it comes to individual Jews. Here the charge does not raise any question of self-doubt; in another context the figures on the Jewish role in the press might create feelings of pride. Rather, the fear is of quite another sort. There is a long history of charges of conspiratorial Jewish dominance, and the climax of this history of anti-Semitism was the Holocaust. Privately, and sometimes publicly, Jews are proud of the fact that a group that represents two or three percent of the American population may comprise a much larger percentage of leading figures in the media. When others point to the same figures, however, we may detect, quite correctly, not the motive of approbation of group accomplishment, but quite a different motive: the desire to arouse hostility toward Jews. The role of Jews in the press may be presented as an example of illicit and illegitimate group power, and this power may be charged with responsibility, for example, for the predominance of news about black social problems in newspapers and television coverage.

Certainly from the point of view of group harmony it would be better if both these topics simply were not raised, along with many other topics. But there is also some degree of legitimacy, depending on motive and style, in raising them. In view of the paltriness of many questions that are raised and researched in the college and university and discussed in the press, popular and scholarly, in view of the fact that these difficult topics raise researchable questions and that many would be interested in the research findings, in view of the fact that there might even be significant policy consequences, how can we say that certain avenues of research should be closed off, not discussed, because the mere raising of them, however tactfully, will arouse self-doubt and fear? It may well be the case that we cannot fault all those who raise these questions on the ground of bad motives—racist attitudes, the desire to stir up trouble between groups, the desire to reduce groups to a subordinate position, or, at the extreme, to wipe them out. Do the consequences of raising and discussing a question, the reaction of those it affects, determine whether we consider the researching of the question legitimate?

I have already given my opinion—and reported the views of constitutional scholars—that we cannot solve this problem in the United States through laws and codes. (I am not suggesting it is solved in other countries through laws and codes, but at least they have greater freedom to pass laws and promulgate codes.) Aside from the limitations of the First Amendment, which receives solid support from public opinion, I would not want to put into the hands of judges decisions as to the motives that prompt certain assertions or publications, decisions as to their consequences for group relations, or decisions as to their truth. Yet these questions of motive, consequences, and truth are of the essence and cannot be ignored. How are they to be dealt with?

I would argue that they are best dealt with in the more limited environments in which they come up, rather than through public law and through the civil and criminal cases that would follow bringing such speech and publication under legal scrutiny. The principle here is that this is not a matter for the U.S. Congress or the Supreme Court; rather, it is a matter for individual communities. Perhaps there is something to be learned here from the confused record of the legal and judicial control of obscenity. One can be sure that the founding fathers never thought of this topic when they drafted the First Amendment, though it came to gain the protection of the Amendment. In time, the Supreme Court adopted the position that community standards could govern the exhibition and sale of pornographic materials. Perhaps this is not so different from what happened in the case of control of alcohol. A national standard, prohibition, was abandoned, and each state and community could decide what it would do to control alcohol. If there is a community with common standards and common goals, then such a devolution of the control of offensive speech to the operating community might well be one possible and partial solution.

I believe that colleges and universities form such communities to some degree. Because I do not think the courts are the right place to resolve these matters, I have taken a particular interest in the cases of Professors Michael Levin and Leonard Jeffries at New York's City College. I will conclude by describing what did happen in these cases and what ideally should have happened. To what degree we can transfer lessons we may learn from the problem of offensive speech and writing raised by faculty members to other contexts is a difficult problem and I will not go into it here. It is enough I think to define an approach to controlling offensive speech in one arena where the issue has come up sharply, the college and university.

The story is as follows. Levin, a tenured professor of philosophy, argued that it was legitimate to treat blacks differently because of the statistics as to black crime (for example, storekeepers afraid young black men might be bent on mischief could keep them out, on the basis of their race). He also argued that blacks are, on average, less intelligent than whites. These positions were presented in a letter to the *New York Times*, a book review in an Australian journal, and a letter to a journal of philosophy, though they apparently did not play a role in his teaching. Levin's classes were invaded by student protestors, the college set up a special class to parallel a course he was giving and invited students who were offended by his views to enroll in it, and a committee was set up to study his publications and actions and consider whether further sanctions should be imposed. Levin sued on the grounds that a state agency (the college is public) was punishing him for free speech. After a trial, his charge was upheld, and the college was enjoined from taking any action against him.

Professor Jeffries was notorious for eccentric views on the superiority of blacks and black civilization, which he taught in his classes in black studies and which he publicized in speeches in various forums. He gave a speech on multicultural education, in which he attacked its critics as Jews hostile to black interests, charged that Jews played a significant role in the slave trade, and that Jews and the Mafia in the movie industry were responsible for demeaning representations of blacks. This speech led to a public uproar. As a result, Jeffries's three-year term as chairman of the Black Studies department was reduced to one year, and the college administration also investigated his performance as chairman. Jeffries also went to federal court, claiming he was being punished for constitutionally protected free speech; a jury and judge upheld his claim, and he was reinstated for the full term as chairman and granted monetary damages. However, in further legal proceedings, he eventually lost on both counts.

In both cases professors who had contributed to intergroup discord were initially exonerated under the expansive protection of the First Amendment. This was a conclusion that could only satisfy constitutional lawyers, for the two cases were very different, when viewed through an academic lens and from the point of view of their relevance to one central objective of college and university, the search for truth. In federal court the question was reduced to only one issue, whether they had been punished for constitutionally protected speech. Objectives that would be dominant or should be dominant in a college or university, the search for truth and the limitation of intergroup discord, became irrelevant. As Justice Jackson said in a famous free speech case, "under our system, there is no such thing as a false idea."[6]

Ideally, these matters should have been dealt with within the university. I realize there is a serious problem in this position. City College overvalued the objective of peace, undervalued the objective of truth. Michael Levin is a serious philosopher who has devoted himself, as a scholar, to the issues that got him into trouble. He deserved protection rather than censure. Jeffries, in contrast, had published nothing in a more-than-twenty-year career at City College and had presented outlandish theories without a shred of support in his classes. He should have been relegated to a position of insignificance long before the sensational speech he made created the storm of protest that forced the college to take some action against him.

The differences were irrelevant to the college administrators. Instead, their response was determined by who could make the most trouble if censured (Levin could make little; Jeffries and his supporters could make much); and the college, in its search for intergroup harmony, a legitimate objective, came down hard on Levin and ignored the fact that Jeffries had created a private fiefdom devoted to outlandish theories in the Black Studies department. Nevertheless, the principle that these were matters for the college as a community of students, faculty, and administrators to deal with by its own standards remains valid. City College was dealing badly with them, and so, reluctantly, one must accept the conclusion that recourse to the courts may be necessary. I would still have preferred the court's deference to institutional autonomy, hoping that in time the constellation of forces in the college would change and the value of the limitation of intergroup conflict could have been counterbalanced by the value of respect for the search for truth, rather than becoming, as it did at City College, the controlling value.

As the Levin and Jeffries cases demonstrate, my preferred approach for dealing with this matter at the community level has its own problems. My tendency is to eschew courts and codes and hope for the achievement of a measure of group harmony through the give-and-take of discussion within communities that accept some common objectives, among them both the desirability of reducing strains in intergroup conflict and the legitimate and disinterested search for truth. This should still be our objective. It requires also moderating our absolutism regarding any single value. It would have been better if Michael Levin had pursued his researches even more quietly than he had, located as he was in a college with a large minority population. It would have been better if Leonard Jeffries had taken account of the great Jewish role in City College, the significant number of alumni who were Jews, the way the Jewish public would respond to his peculiar interest in the Jewish role in the slave trade. A proper balancing of concern for scientific research and truth with concern for intergroup harmony at the college would, I think, have led to such moderation. In saying this, I am assuming, going back to motives, that the motives of both professors did not include the exacerbation of intergroup conflict. If that is what someone intends and wants, then appeal to the common interests of a community, as well as appeal to the common interests of the nation, will do no good. I am convinced, however, that a good deal of what we consider hate speech is based on no such insidious motives. Some is; and then the only response is shunning and isolation.

NOTES

1. Allison Davis, Burleigh B. Gardner, and Mary R. Gardner, *Deep South* (Chicago: University of Chicago Press, 1941), p. 22.

2. Nathan Glazer, "Levin, Jeffries, and the Fate of Academic Autonomy," *The Public Interest* (Summer 1995): 14–40; Tony Martin, *The Jewish Onslaught* (Dover, Mass.: The Majority Press), 1993.

3. Richard J. Herrnstein and Charles Murray, *The Bell Curve: Intelligence and Class Structure in American Life* (New York: The Free Press, 1994).

4. Samuel Walker, *Hate Speech: The History of an American Controversy* (Lincoln, Nebr.: University of Nebraska Press, 1994), pp. 102–3.

5. Mari J. Matsuda et al., *Words That Wound: Critical Race Theory, Assaultive Speech, and the First Amendment* (Boulder, Colo.: Westview Press, 1993), p. 30.

6. Ibid., p. 32.

Index

About the Editors and Contributors

MURRAY FRIEDMAN has been the director of the Myer and Rosaline Feinstein Center for American Jewish History, Temple University, since its inception in 1990. The Feinstein Center is a joint project of Temple University and the Philadelphia Chapter of the American Jewish Committee; Dr. Friedman has been the chapter's director for 39 years. From 1986 to 1989, he held a presidential appointment as vice-chairman of the U.S. Commission on Civil Rights. He is the author of *What Went Wrong: The Creation and Abandonment of the Black–Jewish Alliance* and numerous other publications in the areas of American Jewish History, ethnicity, and intergroup relations.

NANCY ISSERMAN has been the associate director of the Myer and Rosaline Feinstein Center for American Jewish History, Temple University, for the past five years. Prior to this she served as assistant director of the Chicago Chapter of the American Jewish Committee and executive director of the Committee on Decent Unbiased Campaign Tactics (CONDUCT), a campaign watchdog group focused on Chicago local elections. As a consultant to the Philadelphia Chapter of the American Jewish Committee, she is the author of *Status of Women in Jewish Organizations*. She is also associate director of the Transcending Trauma Research Project of Penn Council for Relationships, School of Medicine, University of Pennsylvania, which is exploring how survivors of the Holocaust and their families have coped and rebuilt their lives after their extreme trauma.

NATHAN GLAZER was born in New York City, attended New York City public schools, the City College of New York, the University of Pennsylvania, and Columbia University (Ph.D. in sociology). He was on the staff of *Commentary* magazine for ten years, worked in publishing at Doubleday and Random House, and taught at Bennington College, Smith College, and the University of California, Berkeley, before going to Harvard University in 1968, where he was professor of education and sociology (emeritus since 1993). He is coeditor of the quarterly of public policy *The Public Interest* and has written and edited books on American society, ethnicity and race relations, immigration, and urban problems and social policy. These include *The Lonely Crowd* (with David Riesman and Reuel Denney); *American Judaism*; *Beyond the Melting Pot* (with Daniel Moynihan); *Affirmative Discrimination*; *Ethnic Dilemmas, 1964–1982*; and most recently *We Are All Multiculturalists Now*. He also writes regularly for *The New Republic*, of which he is a contributing editor.

JUDITH GOODE is an urban anthropologist who has worked in Latin America and the United States. For the past fifteen years she has been doing ethnographic studies in Philadelphia among descendants of turn-of-the-century immigrants as well as new immigrants. She is president of the Society for the Anthropology of North America, professor of anthropology at Temple University, and has authored several books and articles.

JAMES DAVISON HUNTER is the William R. Kenan Professor of Sociology and Religious Studies at the University of Virginia and director of the Post-Modernity Project. The author of *Evangelicalism: The Coming Generation, Culture Wars: The Struggle to Define America*, and *Before the Shooting Begins: Searching for Democracy in America's Culture War*, he is continuing his research on the moral foundations of contemporary culture and the meaning of the postmodern reconfiguration of American life. His most recent work deals with the moral education of children.

JAMES KURTH is professor of Political Science at Swarthmore College, where he teaches international politics, comparative politics, and multicultural politics. He has been a visiting professor at Harvard University, the University of California at San Diego, the Institute for Advanced Study at Princeton, and the U.S. Naval War College. His recent publications have focused on ethnic and cultural conflict in the United States and in Europe.

GARY Y. OKIHIRO is a professor of history and director of the Asian American Studies Program at Cornell University. He is author of *Cane Fires: The Anti-Japanese Movement in Hawaii, 1865–1945*, *Margins and Mainstreams: Asians in American History and Culture*, and, with Joan Myers, *Whispered Silences: Japanese Americans and World War II*.

PHILIP PERLMUTTER, until his retirement in 1990, was a community and intergroup relations official with the Jewish Community Relations Council in Boston, the American Jewish Committee, the American Jewish Congress, and the Anti-Defamation League. For three years (1988–1991), he was chairman of the Massachusetts Advisory Committee of the U.S. Commission on Civil Rights. His 1992 book *Divided We Fall: A History of Ethnic, Religious and Racial Prejudice in America* received an "Outstanding Book" citation from the Gustavus Myers Center for the Study of Human Rights. More recently he published *The Dynamics of American Ethnic, Religious and Racial Group Life: An Interdisciplinary Approach* (Praeger, 1996).

JONATHAN RIEDER is professor and chair, Department of Sociology, Barnard College, Columbia University; a member of the graduate faculty, Department of Sociology, Columbia University; and coeditor of *CommonQuest: The Magazine of Black-Jewish Relations*. He has also taught at Swarthmore College and Yale University. The author of the award-winning *Canarsie: The Jews and Italians of Brooklyn against Liberalism*, he is currently completing a book entitled *Righteous Passion in American Politics*. Rieder has written widely on issues of race and ethnicity, black-Jewish relations, politics and language, and culture in contemporary America in both scholarly publications and more popular journals, including *The New York Times Book Review* and *The New Republic* (for which he served as a contributing editor between 1989 and 1994). His many awards and honors include membership in the Institute for Advanced Study at Princeton, a visiting scholar position at the Russell Sage Foundation, and an Andrew Mellon Fellowship at the Aspen Institute for Humanistic Study.

GARY E. RUBIN is assistant executive vice president for policy of the New York Association of New Americans, Inc. (NYANA) and teacher at the School of International and Public Affairs of Columbia University. He was previously director of national affairs for the American Jewish Committee and executive director of Americans for Peace Now, an organization promoting Middle East peace and security. His articles on immigration, intergroup relations, and international affairs have appeared in leading newspapers such as the *Los Angeles Times*, *Newsday*, and the *Christian Science Monitor*, as well as in Anglo-Jewish newspapers across the United States.

KIMON HOWLAND SARGEANT is the Sorokin Post-Doctoral Fellow at the University of Virginia's Post-Modernity Project. He has published several articles on religion and cultural conflict. His forthcoming book *The Consumerist Ethic and the Spirit of Evangelicalism* is a scholarly examination of the Evangelical "seeker" church movement.

STEPHEN STEINLIGHT is the Director of National Affairs at the American Jewish Committee (AJC). Dr. Steinlight is also founder of and Senior Advisor to *CommonQuest: The Magazine of Black/Jewish Relations*, co-sponsored by the AJC and Howard University, and is Consulting Editor of the London-based journal, *Patterns of Prejudice*. Dr. Steinlight has worked with the National Conference (NCCJ), the United States Holocaust Memorial Council, and has taught at the University of Sussex, the Institut Britannique de Paris, the State University of New York, and the Graduate School of New York University.